EDWARD LEAR'S
NONSENSE OMNIBUS

Lear showing a doubting stranger his name in his hat to prove that Edward Lear was a man and not merely a name.

Drawn by Himself.

EDWARD LEAR'S
NONSENSE
OMNIBUS

With all the Original Pictures,
Verses, and Stories of his
BOOK OF NONSENSE
MORE NONSENSE
NONSENSE SONGS
NONSENSE STORIES
AND ALPHABETS

with
Introduction by
SIR E. STRACHEY, BART.

FREDERICK WARNE & CO. LTD.
LONDON AND NEW YORK

First Published in Omnibus style 1943

From the Original Authentic
Editions published by
FREDERICK WARNE & CO. LTD.
LONDON

There was an Old Derry down Derry, Who loved to see little folks merry;
So he made them a book, and with laughter they shook
At the fun of that Derry down Derry.

PRINTED IN GREAT BRITAIN

PUBLISHER'S PREFACE

EDWARD LEAR must always be regarded as one of the most curious figures in English literature. He secured a permanent niche in the Temple of Fame by what he regarded as a mere pastime, till the literary world of the nineteenth century proclaimed its delight in it. He is known as the father of English " Nonsense," but his serious ambition and what he regarded as his serious work was landscape painting.

Born in 1812, Lear was not twenty years of age when he was invited by the Earl of Derby to stay at Knowsley to paint the collection of birds there. He remained at Knowsley four years, and it was during that period that he wrote the nonsensical limericks, illustrated with pen drawings, to amuse the juvenile members of the Earl's family. They were dashed off at odd moments, and so little did he think of them that they were not published till ten years later— 1846. Then the reception accorded to them was extraordinary. All sorts of rumours got about as to their authorship, this being ascribed to Lord Brougham, Lord Derby, and others, and attempts were made to read into them political and personal references. But Lear's fantastic absurdities are as void of symbolic meaning as they are of vulgarity and cynicism; they are nonsense pure and simple, and that is their charm.

In later years Lear issued several additional volumes, forsaking the limerick for songs and lyrics, and even prose, but never losing the whimsicality that was new in English letters.

He died in 1888, and in his long life had several striking tributes paid to him. He was placed by Ruskin at the head of his list of the hundred best authors, and Tennyson, while Poet Laureate, wrote verses: " To E.L." He spent much time travelling in the Near East: and published several volumes of landscape paintings, the result of his travels. At one time he was drawing-master to Queen Victoria.

The Stories, Alphabets, and other items in this volume are taken from *Nonsense Songs and Stories* and *Nonsense Botany and Alphabets.*

INTRODUCTION

BY SIR EDWARD STRACHEY, BART.

WHAT is Nonsense ? I know when you do not
ask me. I know that in infancy it is as the very
air we breathe ; that it cheers and strengthens
us in the long weary working days of manhood ; and
brightens and gladdens our old age. But how can I
bring it within the words of a definition ? If the
question is pressed, I must answer it with another.
What is Sense ? Sense is the recognition, adjustment,
and maintenance of the proper and fitting relations of
the affairs of ordinary life. It is a constitutional tact, a
keeping touch with all around it, rather than a
conscious and deliberate action of the intellect. It
almost seems the mental outcome and expression of
our five senses ; and perhaps it is for this reason, as
well as because the sense of the individual always aims
at keeping itself on the average level of his fellows, that
we usually talk of sense as Common Sense. If we call
it Good Sense, it is to remind ourselves that there is a
right and a wrong in this as in everything human. But
it is not Bad Sense, but Nonsense which is the proper
contrary of Sense. In contradiction to the relations and
harmonies of life, Nonsense sets itself to discover and
bring forward the incongruities of all things within
and without us. For while Sense is, and must remain,
essentially prosaic and commonplace, Nonsense has
proved not to be an equally prosaic and commonplace
negative of Sense, not a mere putting forward of
incongruities and absurdities, but the bringing out a
new and deeper harmony of life in and through its
contradictions. Nonsense in fact, in this use of the

word, has shown itself to be a true work of the imagination, a child of genius, and its writing one of the Fine Arts.

From the days when Aristotle investigated the philosophy of laughter, and Aristophanes gave laughter its fullest—I might say its maddest—expression on the stage at Athens, down to this week's issue of "Punch," Nonsense has asserted and made good its claim to a place among the Arts. It has indeed pressed each of them in turn into its service. Nonsense has found the highest expression of itself in music, painting, sculpture, and every form of poetry and prose. The so-called Nonsense Club, which could count Hogarth and Cowper among its members, must have been worthy of the name, for so we have the "March to Finchley" and "John Gilpin" to testify; but as far as I know, Edward Lear first openly gave Nonsense its due place and honour when he called what he wrote pure and absolute Nonsense, and gave the affix of "Nonsense" to every kind of subject; and while we may say, as Johnson did of Goldsmith, that there was hardly a subject which he did not handle, we may add with Johnson, that there was none that he did not adorn by his handling. His pen and pencil vied with each other in pouring forth new kinds of Nonsense Songs, Nonsense Stories, Nonsense Alphabets, and Nonsense Botany. His visit to India supplied him with matter for what I might call Nonsense Philology and Nonsense Politics; and even since his death I have been able to add two new forms of his Nonsense, an Eclogue with the true classical ring, or the Heraldic Blazon of his Cat Foss; the music to which he set the "Pelican Chorus" and the "Yonghy Bonghy Bò" is worthy of the words to which it is wedded; and those who remember the humourous melancholy with which the old man sat down at the piano to play and sing those songs, will give his Nonsense Music a place too.

But " pure and absolute " as Edward Lear declared his Nonsense to be, he was no mere buffoon. His own sketch of his life, given in another part of this volume, and fully confirmed by all that he has left behind him, shows him to have been a conscientious lover of hard work, from the time when, at the age of fifteen, he began to earn " bread and cheese " by selling his " queer songs and sketches," at prices from ninepence to four shillings. This love of hard work is so characteristic of genius, that a great man has (no doubt with some exaggeration) made the capacity for taking infinite pains a definition of genius itself, while the individual humour which is shown in Lear's pictures is itself the sufficient proof of his genius. He was a landscape painter of individual power. The mere list of the books of Natural History which he illustrated ; of the many and distant lands which, poor and weak in health, he visited ; and his journals and records of these places, " with such a pencil, such a pen," is enormous ; and all this while he was carefully cultivating and training himself in the proper work of an artist, which was the real business of his life. And while it is true that, without all this preparation, the Books of Nonsense could not have been written, it is true also that they are only the outcome and overflow of a life which was no less serious and noble than genial and loving. Like Shakespeare, he understood that all merriment should be held " within the limit of becoming mirth," and this limit he found for himself in his fondness for children,—" he loved to see little folks merry,"—and in that habit of doing conscientious and finished work which characterises the true artist.

He gives an account of the beginning and growth of this work in the Introduction to his " More Nonsense," to which I refer the reader. I have myself said more elsewhere on a subject which has for me a never-ending interest. [1] I will rather here give an account of a visit paid by my son Henry to our old friend :—

"When staying at Cannes at Christmas 1882, I was invited by Mr. Lear to go over to San Remo to spend a few days with him. Mr. Lear's villa was large, and the second he had built ; the first became unbearable to him from a large hotel having been planted in front of it. So he put his new house in a place by the sea, where, as he said, nothing could interrupt his light unless the fishes built. The second house was exactly like the first. This, Mr. Lear explained to me, was necessary, or else Foss, his cat, might not have approved of the new villa. At breakfast the morning after I arrived, this much-thought-of, though semi-tailed, cat jumped in at the window and ate a piece of toast from my hand. This, I found, was considered an event ; when visitors stayed at Villa Tennyson, Foss generally hid himself in the back regions ; but his recognition of me was a sort of ' guinea stamp,' which seemed to please Mr. Lear greatly, and assure him of my fitness to receive the constant acts of kindness he was showing me. Being an art student, my interest in Mr. Lear's painting was as great as in his Nonsense, and I can vividly recall the morning spent in his studio, a large room upstairs. He was then at work on a series of water-colours, and his method seemed to be to dip a brush into a large wide-necked bottle of water-colour, and when he had made one or two touches on the drawing, to carry it to the end of the room and put it on the floor, the performance being repeated till quite a row was arranged across the room. Downstairs he had a gallery lighted from the top, which had many

[1] In the *Quarterly Review* of October 1888 and the *Atlantic Monthly* of May 1894, in the former of which was first given the Second Part of " Mr. and Mrs. Discobbolos," and in the latter the " Eclogue " and " Uncle Arly," and in my " Talk at a Country House " (Houghton, Mifflin & Co., Boston, U.S.A., 1894).

beautiful water-colours along the walls, and one great canvas of Mount Athos, which seemed finished, but which he was always making experiments upon in white chalk. At the end of the gallery stood a huge canvas, I think it was 18 feet long, covered over with lines in squares, but no drawing on it. This, he told me, was to be a picture of Enoch Arden on the desert island. My remark that this would be a great undertaking roused Mr. Lear to declare warmly that an old man should never relax his efforts or fail to attempt great things because he was seventy. I could not, however, but feel that there was some inconsistency between this and his habitually saying he was going to live two years longer, and no more. Mr. Lear as an artist was by sympathy a pre-Raphaelite ; he was not one of the original brotherhood, but considered himself a nephew of the originators of the movement, and he told me he had written to his friend, Sir John Millais, ' My dear aunt, I send you a drawing of my cat to show you how I am getting on.'

" Mr. Lear told me that, as a boy, his voice being a good one, he used to be taken to sing at artists' parties, and he was very proud of once having heard Turner (whose art he worshipped) sing a song. Apparently there was no great matter in the ditty, and the note was very untuneable, for Turner had neither voice nor ear. The refrain Mr. Lear remembered, and used to hum, chuckling to himself, ' And the world goes round a-bound, a-bound.' Mr. Lear told me that he approved of the saying of some one, ' Study the works of the Almighty first, and Turner next.' Once meeting a friend who had stayed in a house where Turner was painting, Mr. Lear anxiously asked, ' Cannot you tell me something the great man said ? ' ' He never said anything,' was the reply.

" Mr. Lear's household arrangements were peculiar. Three brothers, young Albanians,—sons of his old servant Giorgio,—did all the housework and cooking, and the youngest, a youth of seventeen, he looked after with fatherly care. He had taught him to say the Lord's Prayer with him every evening, telling me how he felt it his duty to prevent the young man growing up without religion, and expressing his horror of a godless world.

"Mr. Lear was by temperament melancholy; it was not the grave air assumed by a humourist to give his jokes more point, but a gentle sadness through which his humour shone. He felt keenly the neglect of the world for his pictures, but he seemed anxious to prevent all but his nearest friends seeing them. When I was staying with him, it happened to be the afternoon on which he was supposed to be at home to show his pictures to possible buyers. Early in the afternoon he told me that he sent his servants out, and was going to open the door himself. He explained that if any one came he did not like he could send them away, and also keep out Germans. He seemed to have a great horror and fear that a German might be let in by accident. What caused this fear I was not able to discover. As the afternoon advanced a ring at the door-bell was heard, and Mr. Lear went to open the door. Sitting in the gallery, I heard the voice of a lady inquiring if she could see the pictures, and I could hear Mr. Lear, in a voice of the most melancholy kind, telling her that he never showed his pictures now, he was much too ill; and from his voice and words I have no doubt the lady went away with the idea that a most unhappy man lived there. Mr. Lear came back to the gallery with much satisfaction at the working of his plan, which was so far superior to the servant's ' Not at home,' as by his method he could send away bores and let in people he liked. Later on, some friends he wanted to see came, and the melancholy old man, too ill to show his pictures, changed into the

most genial host. In the evenings he often sang; the
'Yonghy Bonghy Bò' was inimitable. His voice had
gone, but the refinement and expression was remarkable. His touch, too, was finished and smooth;
unfortunately his playing was by ear, so that many of
the really beautiful songs he composed were lost.
One such still haunts me; the words, Tennyson's
'In the Garden at Swainston,' were set to most
touching and appropriate music. I think he felt the
words very strongly; they echoed his own feelings;
he had outlived many friends, and many dead men
'walked in the walks' with him. He showed me a
long frame with photographs of his friends in it; it
hung in the drawing-room, but there were several
blank places. He told me when a friend died his
picture was taken out and put into a frame hanging in
his bedroom. This melancholy never soured his mind
nor stopped his matchless flow of humour and bad
puns; but it coloured them all. My visit at Villa
Tennyson coming to an end, on the last evening after
dinner he wrote a letter for me to take back to my
father, sending him the then unpublished conclusion
to Mr. and Mrs. Discobbolos; and when this was done
he took from a place in his bureau a number of
carefully cut-out backs of old envelopes, and on these
he drew, to send to my sister, then eight years old, the
delightful series of heraldic pictures of his cat. After
he had done seven he said it was a great shame to
caricature Foss, and laid aside the pen.

"The next day ended my visit—one which I shall
ever remember. The touching kindness which marked
all his actions towards me I shall never forget; and I
still see the tall, melancholy form, with loose clothes
and round spectacles, leaning over the railings of the
San Remo railway station, though happily I did not
then know that I was looking on that kindly figure for
the last time.   H. S."

In conclusion, and as counterpart to this account of the good old man and his household, let me commend to the reader the autobiographical sketches, to one of which I have already referred. They were published "By Way of Preface" to a former edition of the present volume and are here reprinted.

EDWARD STRACHEY.

SUTTON COURT, *September* 1894.

BY WAY OF PREFACE

IT is believed that all save the youngest readers of
these Nonsense Books will be interested in the two
following autobiographical letters by the author,
which have never till now been published. The first,
written nearly a quarter of a century back, just before
one of his journeys in search of the picturesque, is a
strict recital of date and fact ; the second, composed
some years later, and after he had set up his residence
at San Remo, was written for a young lady of his
acquaintance, who had quoted to him the words of a
young lady not of his acquaintance, which form the
refrain of the verses—" How pleasant to know
Mr. Lear ! "

My Dear F.,

I want to send you, before leaving England, a note
or two as to the various publications I have uttered,—
bad and good, and of all sorts,—also their dates, that
so you might be able to screw them into a beautiful
memoir of me in case I leave my bones at Palmyra or
elsewhere. Leastwise, if a man does anything all
through life with a deal of bother, and likewise of some
benefit to others, the details of such bother and benefit
may as well be known accurately as the contrary.

Born in 1812 (12th May), I began to draw, for bread and cheese, about 1827, but only did uncommon queer shop-sketches—selling them for prices varying from ninepence to four shillings : colouring prints, screens, fans ; awhile making morbid disease drawings for hospitals and certain doctors of physic. In 1831, through Mrs. Wentworth, I became employed at the Zoological Society, and, in 1832, published "The Family of the Psittacidæ," the first complete volume of coloured drawings of birds on so large a scale published in England, as far as I know—unless Audubon's were previously engraved. J. Gould's "Indian Pheasants" were commenced at the same time, and after a little while he employed me to draw many of his birds of Europe, while I assisted Mrs. Gould in all her drawings of foregrounds, as may be seen in a moment by any one who will glance at my drawings in G.'s European birds and the Toucans. From 1832 to 1836, when my health failed a good deal, I drew much at the Earl of Derby's ; and a series of my drawings was published by Dr. Gray of the British Museum—a book now rare. I also lithographed many various detached subjects, and a large series of Testudinata for Mr. (now Professor) Bell ; and I made drawings for Bell's "British Mammalia," and for two or more volumes of the "Naturalist's Library " for the editor, Sir W. Jardine, those volumes being the Parrots, and, I think, the Monkeys, and some Cats. In 1835 or '36, being in Ireland and the Lakes, I leaned more and more to landscape, and when in 1837 it was found that my health was more affected by the climate month by month, I went abroad, wintering in Rome till 1841, when I came to England and published a volume of lithographs called "Rome and its Environs." Returning to Rome, I visited Sicily and much of the South of Italy, and continued to make chalk drawings, though in 1840 I had painted my two first oil-paintings. I also gave lessons in drawing at Rome, and was able to make a very comfortable living. In 1845 I came again to England, and in 1846 gave Queen Victoria some lessons, through Her Majesty's having seen a work I published in that year on the Abruzzi, and another on the Roman States. In 1847 I went through all Southern Calabria, and again went round Sicily, and in 1848 left Rome entirely. I travelled then to Malta, Greece, Constantinople, and the Ionian Islands; and to Mount Sinai and Greece a second time in 1849, returning to England in that year. All 1850 I gave up to improving myself in figure-drawing, and I continued to paint oil-paintings till 1853, having published in the meantime, in 1849 and 1852, two volumes entitled "Journals of a Landscape Painter," in Albania and Calabria. The first edition of the "Book of Nonsense" was published in 1846, lithographed by tracing-paper. In 1854 I went to Egypt and Switzerland, and in 1855 to Corfu, where I remained the winters of 1856-57-58, visiting Athos, and, later, Jerusalem and Syria. In the autumn of 1858 I returned to England, and '59 and '60 winters were passed in Rome. 1861, I remained all the winter in England, and painted the Cedars of Lebanon and Masada, going, after my sister's death

in March 1861, to Italy. The two following winters—
'62 and '63—were passed at Corfu, and in the end of
the latter year I published " Views in the Ionian
Islands." In 1862 a second edition of the " Book of
Nonsense," much enlarged, was published, and is
now in its sixteenth thousand.

O bother !

Yours affectionately,

EDWARD LEAR.

" How pleasant to know Mr. Lear ! "
   Who has written such volumes of stuff !
Some think him ill-tempered and queer,
   But a few think him pleasant enough.

His mind is concrete and fastidious,
   His nose is remarkably big ;
His visage is more or less hideous,
   His beard it resembles a wig.

He has ears, and two eyes, and ten fingers,
   Leastways if you reckon two thumbs ;
Long ago he was one of the singers,
   But now he is one of the dumbs.

He sits in a beautiful parlour,
   With hundreds of books on the wall ;
He drinks a great deal of Marsala,
   But never gets tipsy at all.

He has many friends, laymen and clerical,
   Old Foss is the name of his cat :
His body is perfectly spherical,
   He weareth a runcible hat.

When he walks in a waterproof white,
   The children run after him so !
Calling out, " He's come out in his night-
   gown, that crazy old Englishman, oh ! "

He weeps by the side of the ocean,
   He weeps on the top of the hill ;
He purchases pancakes and lotion,
   And chocolate shrimps from the mill.

He reads but he cannot speak Spanish,
   He cannot abide ginger-beer :
Ere the days of his pilgrimage vanish,
   How pleasant to know Mr. Lear !

CONTENTS

CONTENTS

CONTENTS

CONTENTS

THE BOOK OF NONSENSE

Dedication

—

There was an Old Man with a beard,
Who said, "It is just as I feared!—
      Two Owls and a Hen,
      Four Larks and a Wren,
Have all built their nests in my beard!"

There was a Young Lady of Ryde,
Whose shoe-strings were seldom untied.
　　She purchased some clogs,
　　And some small spotted dogs,
And frequently walked about Ryde.

There was an Old Man with a nose,
Who said, " If you choose to suppose
    That my nose is too long,
     You are certainly wrong ! "
That remarkable man with a nose.

There was an Old Man on a hill,
Who seldom, if ever, stood still;
   He ran up and down
   In his grandmother's gown,
Which adorned that Old Man on a hill.

There was a Young Lady whose bonnet
Came untied when the birds sat upon it;
    But she said, " I don't care !
    All the birds in the air
Are welcome to sit on my bonnet ! "

B

There was a Young Person of Smyrna,
Whose grandmother threatened to burn her;
    But she seized on the cat,
    And said, " Granny, burn that!
You incongruous old woman of Smyrna!"

There was an Old Person of Chili,
Whose conduct was painful and silly ;
    He sat on the stairs
     Eating apples and pears,
That imprudent Old Person of Chili.

There was an Old Man with a gong,
Who bumped at it all the day long ;
    But they called out, " Oh, law !
    You're a horrid old bore ! "
So they smashed that Old Man with a gong.

There was an Old Lady of Chertsey,
Who made a remarkable curtsey;
    She twirled round and round
    Till she sank underground,
Which distressed all the people of Chertsey.

There was an Old Man in a tree,
Who was horribly bored by a bee ;
    When they said, " Does it buzz ? "
    He replied, " Yes, it does !
It's a regular brute of a bee ! "

There was an Old Man with a flute.
A " sarpint " ran into his boot;
   But he played day and night,
   Till the " sarpint " took flight,
And avoided that man with a flute.

There was a Young Lady whose chin
Resembled the point of a pin ;
 So she had it made sharp,
 And purchased a harp,
And played several tunes with her chin.

There was an Old Man of Kilkenny,
Who never had more than a penny ;
　　He spent all that money
　　In onions and honey,
That wayward Old Man of Kilkenny.

B*

There was an Old Person of Ischia,
Whose conduct grew friskier and friskier;
    He danced hornpipes and jigs,
    And ate thousands of figs,
That lively Old Person of Ischia.

There was an Old Man in a boat,
Who said, " I'm afloat ! I'm afloat ! "
　　When they said, " No, you ain't ! "
　　He was ready to faint,
That unhappy Old Man in a boat.

There was a Young Lady of Portugal,
Whose ideas were excessively nautical;
    She climbed up a tree
    To examine the sea,
But declared she would never leave Portugal.

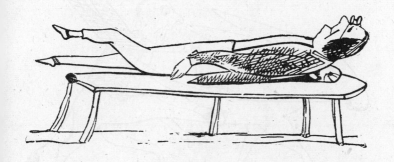

There was an Old Man of Moldavia,
Who had the most curious behaviour;
　　For while he was able
　　He slept on a table,
That funny Old Man of Moldavia.

There was an Old Man of Madras,
Who rode on a cream-coloured ass ;
    But the length of its ears
    So promoted his fears,
That it killed that Old Man of Madras.

There was an Old Person of Leeds,
Whose head was infested with beads;
    She sat on a stool
    And ate gooseberry-fool,
Which agreed with that Person of Leeds.

There was an Old Person of Hurst,
Who drank when he was not athirst;
  When they said, " You'll grow fatter ! "
  He answered, " What matter ? "
That globular Person of Hurst.

There was a Young Person of Crete,
Whose toilet was far from complete;
  She dressed in a sack
  Spickle-speckled with black,
That ombliferous Person of Crete.

There was an Old Man of the Isles,
Whose face was pervaded with smiles ;
   He sung " High dum diddle,"
   And played on the fiddle,
That amiable man of the Isles.

There was an Old Person of Buda,
Whose conduct grew ruder and ruder,
    Till at last with a hammer
    They silenced his clamour,
By smashing that Person of Buda.

There was an Old Man of Columbia,
Who was thirsty and called out for some beer!
    But they brought it quite hot
    In a small copper pot,
Which disgusted that Man of Columbia.

There was a Young Lady of Dorking,
Who bought a large bonnet for walking;
    But its colour and size
    So bedazzled her eyes,
That she very soon went back to Dorking.

There was an Old Man who supposed
That the street door was partially closed ;
    But some very large rats
    Ate his coats and his hats,
While that futile Old Gentleman dozed.

There was an Old Man of the West,
Who wore a pale plum-coloured vest ;
    When they said, " Does it fit ? "
    He replied, " Not a bit ! "
That uneasy Old Man of the West.

There was an Old Man of the Wrekin,
Whose shoes made a horrible creaking;
    But they said, " Tell us whether
    Your shoes are of leather,
Or of what, you Old Man of the Wrekin ? "

There was a Young Lady whose eyes
Were unique as to colour and size ;
    When she opened them wide,
    People all turned aside,
And started away in surprise.

There was a Young Lady of Norway,
Who casually sat in a doorway;
 When the door squeezed her flat,
 She exclaimed, "What of that?"
This courageous Young Lady of Norway.

There was an Old Man of Vienna,
Who lived upon tincture of senna ;
When that did not agree
He took camomile tea,
That nasty Old Man of Vienna.

There was an Old Person whose habits
Induced him to feed upon rabbits;
    When he'd eaten eighteen
    He turned perfectly green,
Upon which he relinquished those habits.

There was an Old Person of Dover,
Who rushed through a field of blue clover;
    But some very large bees
    Stung his nose and his knees,
So he very soon went back to Dover.

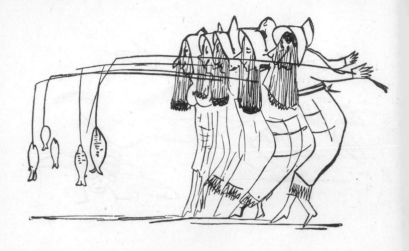

There was an Old Man of Marseilles,
Whose daughters wore bottle-green veils;
    They caught several fish,
    Which they put in a dish,
And sent to their Pa at Marseilles.

There was an Old Person of Cadiz,
Who was always polite to the ladies;
    But in handing his daughter,
    He fell into the water,
Which drowned that Old Person of Cadiz.

There was an Old Person of Basing,
Whose presence of mind was amazing;
　　He purchased a steed,
　　Which he rode at full speed,
And escaped from the people of Basing.

There was an Old Man of Quebec,—
A beetle ran over his neck;
     But he cried, " With a needle
     I'll slay you, O beadle ! "
That angry Old Man of Quebec.

C

There was an Old Person of Philæ,
Whose conduct was dubious and wily;
    He rushed up a palm
    When the weather was calm,
And observed all the ruins of Philæ.

There was a Young Lady of Bute,
Who played on a silver-gilt flute;
    She played several jigs
    To her uncle's white pigs,
That amusing Young Lady of Bute.

There was a Young Lady whose nose
Was so long that it reached to her toes ;
    So she hired an old lady,
    Whose conduct was steady,
To carry that wonderful nose.

There was an Old Man of Apulia,
Whose conduct was very peculiar;
    He fed twenty sons
    Upon nothing but buns,
That whimsical Man of Apulia.

There was an Old Man with a poker,
Who painted his face with red ochre;
    When they said, " You're a Guy ! "
    He made no reply,
But knocked them all down with his poker.

There was an Old Person of Prague,
Who was suddenly seized with the plague ;
　　But they gave him some butter,
　　Which caused him to mutter,
And cured that Old Person of Prague.

There was an Old Man of the North,
Who fell into a basin of broth;
    But a laudable cook
    Fished him out with a hook,
Which saved that Old Man of the North.

There was an Old Person of Mold,
Who shrank from sensations of cold ;
    So he purchased some muffs,
    Some furs, and some fluffs,
And wrapped himself up from the cold.

c*

There was an Old Man of Nepaul,
From his horse had a terrible fall ;
    But, though split quite in two,
    With some very strong glue
They mended that Man of Nepaul.

There was an Old Man of th' Abruzzi,
So blind that he couldn't his foot see;
    When they said, " That's your toe ! "
    He replied, " Is it so ? "
That doubtful Old Man of th' Abruzzi.

There was an Old Person of Rhodes,
Who strongly objected to toads;
   He paid several cousins
    To catch them by dozens,
That futile Old Person of Rhodes.

There was an Old Man of Peru,
Who watched his wife making a stew;
    But once by mistake,
    In a stove she did bake
That unfortunate Man of Peru.

There was an Old Man of Melrose,
Who walked on the tips of his toes;
    But they said, " It ain't pleasant
    To see you at present,
You stupid Old Man of Melrose."

There was a Young Lady of Lucca,
Whose lovers completely forsook her;
    She ran up a tree,
    And said, " Fiddle-de-dee ! "
Which embarrassed the people of Lucca.

There was an Old Man of Bohemia,
Whose daughter was christened Euphemia;
    But one day, to his grief,
    She married a thief,
Which grieved that Old Man of Bohemia.

There was an Old Man of Vesuvius,
Who studied the works of Vitruvius;
    When the flames burnt his book,
    To drinking he took,
That Morbid Old Man of Vesuvius.

There was an Old Man of Cape Horn,
Who wished he had never been born;
    So he sat on a chair,
    Till he died of despair,
That dolorous Man of Cape Horn.

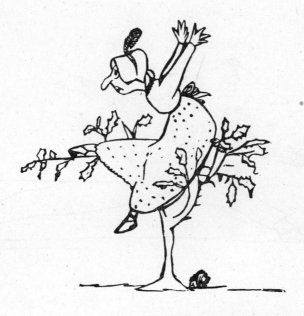

There was an Old Lady whose folly
Induced her to sit in a holly ;
    Whereupon, by a thorn
    Her dress being torn,
She quickly became melancholy.

There was an Old Man of Corfu,
Who never knew what he should do;
So he rushed up and down
Till the sun made him brown,
That bewildered Old Man of Corfu.

There was an Old Man of the South,
Who had an immoderate mouth;
　　But in swallowing a dish,
　　That was quite full of fish,
He was choked, that Old Man of the South.

There was an Old Man of the Nile,
Who sharpened his nails with a file,
    Till he cut off his thumbs,
    And said calmly, " This comes
Of sharpening one's nails with a file! "

There was an Old Person of Rheims,
Who was troubled with horrible dreams;
 So, to keep him awake,
 They fed him on cake,
Which amused that Old Person of Rheims.

There was an Old Person of Cromer,
Who stood on one leg to read Homer;
    When he found he grew stiff,
    He jumped over the cliff,
Which concluded that Person of Cromer.

There was an Old Person of Troy,
Whose drink was warm brandy and soy,
    Which he took with a spoon,
    By the light of the moon,
In sight of the city of Troy.

There was an Old Man of the Dee,
Who was sadly annoyed by a flea ;
    When he said, " I will scratch it,"
    They gave him a hatchet,
Which grieved that Old Man of the Dee.

There was an Old Man of Dundee,
Who frequented the top of a tree;
    When disturbed by the crows,
    He abruptly arose,
And exclaimed, " I'll return to Dundee."

There was an Old Person of Tring,
Who embellished his nose with a ring;
    He gazed at the moon
    Every evening in June,
That ecstatic Old Person of Tring.

There was an Old Man on some rocks,
Who shut his wife up in a box;
    When she said, "Let me out!"
    He exclaimed, "Without doubt,
You will pass all your life in that box."

There was an Old Man of Coblenz,
The length of whose legs was immense;
    He went with one prance
    From Turkey to France,
That surprising Old Man of Coblenz.

There was an Old Man of Calcutta,
Who perpetually ate bread and butter,
 Till a great bit of muffin,
 On which he was stuffing,
Choked that horrid Old Man of Calcutta.

There was an Old Man in a pew,
Whose waistcoat was spotted with blue ;
    But he tore it in pieces
    To give to his nieces,
That cheerful Old Man in a pew.

There was an Old Man who said, " How
Shall I flee from that horrible cow ?
    I will sit on this stile,
    And continue to smile,
Which may soften the heart of that cow."

D

There was a Young Lady of Hull,
Who was chased by a virulent bull;
    But she seized on a spade,
      And called out, " Who's afraid ? "
Which distracted that virulent bull.

There was an Old Man of Whitehaven,
Who danced a quadrille with a raven ;
    But they said, " It's absurd
    To encourage this bird ! "
So they smashed that Old Man of Whitehaven.

There was an Old Man of Leghorn,
The smallest that ever was born;
    But quickly snapped up he
    Was once by a puppy,
Who devoured that Old Man of Leghorn.

There was an Old Man of the Hague,
Whose ideas were excessively vague;
　　He built a balloon
　　To examine the moon,
That deluded Old Man of the Hague.

There was an Old Man of Jamaica,
Who suddenly married a Quaker;
    But she cried out, " Alack !
    I have married a black ! "
Which distressed that Old Man of Jamaica.

There was an Old Person of Dutton,
Whose head was as small as a button,
　　So, to make it look big,
　　He purchased a wig,
And rapidly rushed about Dutton.

There was a Young Lady of Tyre,
Who swept the loud chords of a lyre;
    At the sound of each sweep
    She enraptured the deep,
And enchanted the city of Tyre.

There was an Old Man who said, " Hush !
I perceive a young bird in this bush ! "
    When they said, " Is it small ? "
    He replied, " Not at all !
It is four times as big as the bush ! "

D*

There was an Old Man of the East,
Who gave all his children a feast;
    But they all ate so much,
    And their conduct was such
That it killed that Old Man of the East.

There was an Old Man of Kamschatka,
Who possessed a remarkably fat cur;
    His gait and his waddle
    Were held as a model
To all the fat dogs in Kamschatka.

There was an Old Man of the coast,
Who placidly sat on a post;
    But when it was cold
    He relinquished his hold
And called for some hot buttered toast.

There was an Old Person of Bangor,
Whose face was distorted with anger!
    He tore off his boots,
    And subsisted on roots,
That irascible Person of Bangor.

There was an Old Man with a beard,
Who sat on a horse when he reared ;
　　But they said, " Never mind !
　　You will fall off behind,
You propitious Old Man with a beard ! "

There was an Old Man of the West,
Who never could get any rest;
    So they set him to spin
    On his nose and his chin,
Which cured that Old Man of the West.

There was an Old Person of Anerley,
Whose conduct was strange and unmannerly;
　　He rushed down the Strand
　　With a pig in each hand,
But returned in the evening to Anerley.

There was a Young Lady of Troy,
Whom several large flies did annoy;
 Some she killed with a thump,
 Some she drowned at the pump,
And some she took with her to Troy.

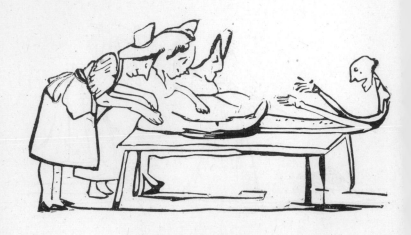

There was an Old Man of Berlin,
Whose form was uncommonly thin ;
   Till he once, by mistake,
   Was mixed up in a cake,
So they baked that Old Man of Berlin.

There was an Old Person of Spain,
Who hated all trouble and pain ;
    So he sat on a chair,
    With his feet in the air,
That umbrageous Old Person of Spain.

There was a Young Lady of Russia,
Who screamed so that no one could hush her;
    Her screams were extreme,—
    No one heard such a scream
As was screamed by that Lady of Russia.

There was an Old Man who said, " Well !
Will *nobody* answer this bell ?
    I have pulled day and night,
    Till my hair has grown white,
But nobody answers this bell ! "

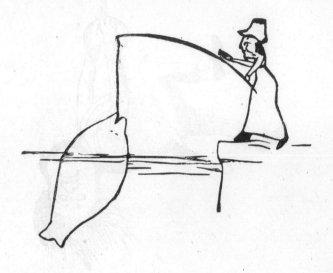

There was a Young Lady of Wales,
Who caught a large fish without scales;
    When she lifted her hook
      She exclaimed, " Only look ! "
That ecstatic Young Lady of Wales.

There was an Old Person of Cheadle,
Who was put in the stocks by the beadle
    For stealing some pigs,
      Some coats, and some wigs,
That horrible Person of Cheadle.

There was a Young Lady of Welling,
Whose praise all the world was a-telling;
    She played on a harp,
    And caught several carp,
That accomplished Young Lady of Welling.

There was an Old Person of Tartary,
Who divided his jugular artery ;
    But he screeched to his wife,
    And she said, " Oh, my life !
Your death will be felt by all Tartary ! "

There was an Old Person of Chester,
Whom several small children did pester ;
    They threw some large stones,
    Which broke most of his bones,
And displeased that Old Person of Chester.

There was an Old Man with an owl,
Who continued to bother and howl;
    He sat on a rail
    And imbibed bitter ale,
Which refreshed that Old Man and his owl.

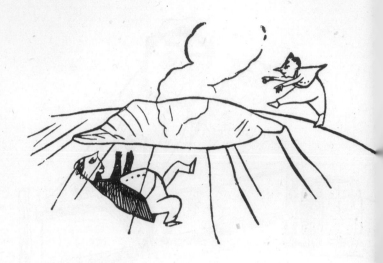

There was an Old Person of Gretna,
Who rushed down the crater of Etna ;
    When they said, " Is it hot ? "
    He replied, " No, it's not ! "
That mendacious Old Person of Gretna.

There was a Young Lady of Sweden,
Who went by the slow train to Weedon;
    When they cried, " Weedon Station ! "
    She made no observation,
But thought she should go back to Sweden.

There was a Young Girl of Majorca,
Whose aunt was a very fast walker;
   She walked seventy miles,
   And leaped fifteen stiles,
Which astonished that Girl of Majorca.

There was an Old Man of the Cape,
Who possessed a large Barbary ape,
　　Till the ape one dark night
　　Set the house all alight,
Which burned that Old Man of the Cape.

There was an Old Lady of Prague,
Whose language was horribly vague;
    When they said, " Are these caps ? "
    She answered, " Perhaps ! "
That oracular Lady of Prague.

There was an Old Person of Sparta,
Who had twenty-five sons and one " darter ";
    He fed them on snails,
    And weighed them in scales,
That wonderful Person of Sparta.

E

There was an Old Man at a casement,
Who held up his hands in amazement;
    When they said, " Sir, you'll fall ! "
    He replied, " Not at all ! "
That incipient Old Man at a casement.

There was a Young Lady of Clare,
Who was sadly pursued by a bear ;
    When she found she was tired,
    She abruptly expired,
That unfortunate Lady of Clare.

There was an Old Person of Ems,
Who casually fell in the Thames;
    And when he was found
    They said he was drowned,
That unlucky Old Person of Ems.

There was an Old Man on whose nose,
Most birds of the air could repose;
    But they all flew away
    At the closing of day,
Which relieved that Old Man and his nose.

There was a Young Lady of Parma,
Whose conduct grew calmer and calmer ;
  When they said, " Are you dumb ? "
  She merely said, " Hum ! "
That provoking Young Lady of Parma.

There was an Old Person of Burton,
Whose answers were rather uncertain;
    When they said, " How d'ye do ? "
    He replied, " Who are you ? "
That distressing Old Person of Burton.

There was an Old Man of Aosta,
Who possessed a large cow, but he lost her;
 But they said, " Don't you see
 She has rushed up a tree?
You invidious Old Man of Aosta! "

There was an Old Person of Ewell,
Who chiefly subsisted on gruel;
    But to make it more nice
    He inserted some mice,
Which refreshed that Old Person of Ewell.

E*

MORE NONSENSE

INTRODUCTION

IN offering this little book to the public, I am glad to take the opportunity of recording the pleasure I have received at the appreciation its predecessor has met with, as attested by its wide circulation, and by the universally kind notices of it from the press. To have been the means of administering innocent mirth to thousands, may surely be a just motive for satisfaction, and an excuse for grateful expression.

At the same time I am desirous of adding a few words as to the history of the previously published volume, viz., the first or original " Book of Nonsense," relating to which many absurd reports have crept into circulation, such as that it was the composition of the late Lord Brougham, the late Earl of Derby, etc. ; that the rhymes and pictures are by different persons ; or that the whole have a symbolical meaning, etc. ; whereas, every one of the Rhymes was composed by myself, and every one of the Illustrations drawn by my own hand at the time the verses were made. Moreover, in no portion of these Nonsense drawings have I ever allowed any caricature of private or public persons to appear, and throughout, more care than might be supposed has been given to make the subjects incapable of misinterpretation : " Nonsense," pure and absolute, having been my aim throughout.

As for the persistently absurd report of the late Earl of Derby being the author of the first " Book of Nonsense," I may relate an incident which occurred to me four summers ago, the first that gave me any insight into the origin of the rumour.

I was on my way from London to Guildford, in a railway carriage, containing, besides myself, one passenger, an elderly gentleman. Presently, however, two ladies entered, accompanied by two little boys. These, who had just had a copy of the " Book of Nonsense " given them, were loud in their delight, and by degrees infected the whole party with their mirth.

" How grateful," said the old gentleman to the two ladies, " all children, and parents too, ought to be to the statesman who has given his time to composing that charming book ! "

(The ladies looked puzzled, as indeed was I, the author.)

" Do you not know who is the writer of it ? " asked the gentleman.

" The name is ' Edward Lear,' " said one of the ladies.

" Ah," said the first speaker, " so it is printed ; but that is only a whim of the real author, the Earl of Derby. ' Edward ' is his Christian name, and, as you may see, LEAR is only EARL transposed."

" But," said the lady doubtingly, " here is a dedication to the great-grandchildren, grand-nephews, and grand-nieces of Edward, thirteenth Earl of Derby, by the author, Edward Lear."

" That," replied the other, " is simply a piece of mystification ; I am in a position to know that the whole book was composed and illustrated by Lord Derby himself. In fact, there is no such a person at all as Edward Lear."

" Yet," said the other lady, " some friends of mine tell me they know Mr. Lear."

" Quite a mistake ! Completely a mistake ! " said the old gentleman, becoming rather angry at the contradiction. " I am well aware of what I am saying. I can inform you, no such person as ' Edward Lear ' exists ! "

Hitherto I had kept silence ; but as my hat was, as well as my handkerchief and stick, largely marked inside with my name, and as I happened to have in my pocket several letters addressed to me, the temptation was too great to resist ; so, flashing all these articles at once on my would-be extinguisher's attention, I speedily reduced him to silence.

Long years ago, in days when much of my time was passed in a country house, where children and mirth abounded, the lines beginning, " There was an old man of Tobago," were suggested to me by a valued friend, as a form of verse lending itself to limitless variety for Rhymes and Pictures ; and thenceforth the greater part of the original drawings and verses for the first " Book of Nonsense " were struck off with a pen, no assistance ever having been given me in any way but that of uproarious delight and welcome at the appearance of every new absurdity.

Most of these Drawings and Rhymes were reproduced and issued in the original "Book of Nonsense." But many editions of that work having been exhausted, and the call for it still continuing, I added a considerable number of subjects to those previously published, and these form the present volume.

EDWARD LEAR.

VILLA EMILY, SAN REMO.

There was a Young Person of Bantry,
Who frequently slept in the pantry;
    When disturbed by the mice,
    She appeased them with rice,
That judicious Young Person of Bantry.

There was an Old Man at a Junction,
Whose feelings were wrung with compunction,
    When they said, " The train's gone ! "
    He exclaimed, " How forlorn ! "
But remained on the rails of the Junction.

There was an Old Man, who when little
Fell casually into a Kettle ;
  But, growing too stout,
  He could never get out,
So he passed all his life in that Kettle.

There was an Old Man whose despair
Induced him to purchase a Hare ;
    Whereon one fine day,
    He rode wholly away,
Which partly assuaged his despair.

There was an Old Person of Minety,
Who purchased five hundred and ninety
    Large apples and pears,
     Which he threw unawares,
At the heads of the people of Minety.

There was an Old Man of Thermopylæ,
Who never did anything properly;
    But they said, "If you choose
    To boil Eggs in your Shoes,
You shall never remain in Thermopylæ.

There was an Old Person of Deal,
Who in walking used only his heel;
    When they said, " Tell us why ? "—
    He made no reply;
That mysterious Old Person of Deal.

There was an Old Man on the Humber,
Who dined on a cake of Burnt Umber;
　　When he said, " It's enough ! "—
　　They only said, " Stuff !
You amazing Old Man on the Humber ! "

There was an Old Man of Blackheath,
Whose head was adorned with a Wreath,
    Of lobsters and spice,
    Pickled onions and mice,
That uncommon Old Man of Blackheath.

There was an Old Man of Toulouse,
Who purchased a new pair of Shoes ;
    When they asked, " Are they pleasant ? "—
    He said, " Not at present ! "
That turbid Old Man of Toulouse.

There was an Old Person in Black,
A Grasshopper jumped on his back;
    When it chirped in his ear,
    He was smitten with fear,
That helpless Old Person in Black.

There was an Old Man in a Barge,
Whose Nose was exceedingly large;
    But in fishing by night,
    It supported a light,
Which helped that Old Man in a Barge.

There was an Old Man of Dunrose;
A Parrot seized hold of his Nose.
When he grew melancholy,
They said, " His name's Polly,"
Which soothed that Old Man of Dunrose.

There was an Old Person of Bromley,
Whose ways were not cheerful or comely;
    He sate in the dust,
    Eating Spiders and Crust,
That unpleasing Old Person of Bromley.

There was an Old Man of Dunluce,
Who went out to sea on a Goose;
     When he'd gone out a mile,
     He observ'd with a smile,
" It is time to return to Dunluce."

There was an Old Person of Pinner,
As thin as a lath, if not thinner ;
　　They dressed him in white,
　　And roll'd him up tight,
That elastic Old Person of Pinner.

There was an Old Man in a Marsh,
Whose manners were futile and harsh;
    He sate on a Log,
    And sang Songs to a Frog,
That instructive Old Man in a Marsh.

F

There was an Old Man of Dee-side,
Whose Hat was exceedingly wide ;
    But he said, " Do not fail,
    If it happen to hail,
To come under my Hat at Dee-side ! "

There was an Old Person of Bree,
Who frequented the depths of the Sea;
    She nurs'd the small fishes,
    And washed all the dishes,
And swam back again into Bree.

There was a Young Person in Green,
Who seldom was fit to be seen ;
    She wore a long shawl,
    Over bonnet and all,
Which enveloped that Person in Green.

There was an Old Person of Wick,
Who said, " Tick-a-Tick, Tick-a-Tick ;
   Chickabee, Chickabaw."
   And he said nothing more,
That laconic Old Person of Wick.

There was an Old Man at a Station,
Who made a promiscuous Oration;
　　But they said, " Take some snuff !—
　　You have talk'd quite enough,
You afflicting Old Man at a Station ! "

There was an Old Man of Three Bridges,
Whose mind was distracted by Midges;
    He sate on a wheel,
    Eating underdone Veal,
Which relieved that Old Man of Three Bridges.

There was an Old Person of Fife,
Who was greatly disgusted with life;
    They sang him a ballad,
    And fed him on Salad,
Which cured that Old Person of Fife.

There was an Old Person of Shields,
Who frequented the valleys and fields;
    All the mice and the cats,
    And the snakes and the rats,
Followed after that Person of Shields.

There was an Old Person of China,
Whose daughters were Jiska and Dinah,
    Amelia and Fluffy,
    Olivia and Chuffy,
And all of them settled in China.

There was an Old Man of the Dargle,
Who purchased six barrels of Gargle;
    For he said, " I'll sit still,
    And will roll them down hill,
For the fish in the depths of the Dargle."

There was an Old Man who screamed out
Whenever they knocked him about;
    So they took off his boots,
    And fed him with fruits,
And continued to knock him about.

There was an Old Person of Brill,
Who purchased a Shirt with a Frill;
    But they said, " Don't you wish
    You mayn't look like a fish,
You obsequious Old Person of Brill? "

There was an Old Person of Slough,
Who danced at the end of a Bough;
    But they said, " If you sneeze,
    You might damage the trees,
You imprudent Old Person of Slough."

There was a Young Person in Red,
Who carefully covered her Head,
    With a bonnet of leather,
    And three lines of feather,
Besides some long ribands of red.

There was a Young Person in Pink,
Who called out for something to drink;
　　But they said, " O my daughter,
　　There's nothing but water!"
Which vexed that Young Person in Pink.

There was a Young Lady in White,
Who looked out at the depths of the Night;
  But the birds of the air,
  Filled her heart with despair,
And oppressed that Young Lady in White.

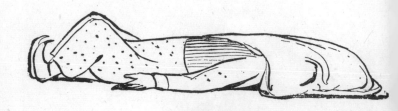

There was an Old Man of Hong Kong,
Who never did anything wrong;
    He lay on his back,
    With his head in a sack,
That innocuous Old Man of Hong Kong.

There was an Old Person of Putney,
Whose food was roast spiders and chutney,
  Which he took with his tea,
  Within sight of the sea,
That romantic Old Person of Putney.

There was an Old Person of Woking,
Whose mind was perverse and provoking;
 He sate on a rail,
 With his head in a Pail,
That illusive Old Person of Woking.

There was an Old Lady of France,
Who taught little Ducklings to dance;
    When she said, " Tick-a-tack ! "—
    They only said, " Quack ! "
Which grieved that Old Lady of France.

There was a Young Lady in Blue,
Who said, " Is it you ? Is it you ? "
    When they said, " Yes, it is,"—
    She replied only, " Whizz ! "
That ungracious Young Lady in Blue.

There was an Old Man in a Garden,
Who always begged every one's pardon,
    When they asked him, " What for ? "—
    He replied, " You're a bore !
And I trust you'll go out of my garden."

There was an Old Person of Loo,
Who said, " What on earth shall I do ? "
    When they said, " Go away ! "—
    She continued to stay,
That vexatious Old Person of Loo.

There was an Old Person of Pisa,
Whose daughters did nothing to please her;
    She dressed them in grey,
    And banged them all day,
Round the walls of the city of Pisa.

There was an Old Person of Florence,
Who held Mutton Chops in abhorrence;
    He purchased a Bustard,
    And fried him in Mustard,
Which choked that Old Person of Florence.

There was an Old Person of Sheen,
Whose expression was calm and serene;
   He sate in the water,
    And drank bottled porter,
That placid Old Person of Sheen.

There was an Old Person of Ware,
Who rode on the back of a Bear;
    When they ask'd, " Does it trot ? "—
    He said, " Certainly not !
He's a Moppsikon Floppsikon Bear ! "

There was an Old Person of Dean,
Who dined on one Pea and one Bean;
   For he said, "More than that
   Would make me too fat,"
That cautious Old Person of Dean.

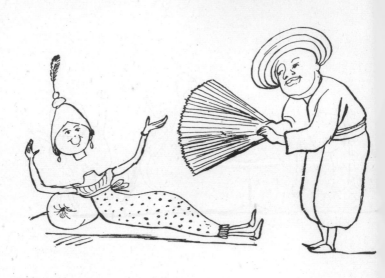

There was a Young Person of Janina,
Whose uncle was always a-fanning her;
When he fanned off her head,
She smiled sweetly and said,
" You propitious Old Person of Janina ! "

There was an Old Person of Down,
Whose face was adorned with a frown;
   When he opened the door,
   For one minute or more,
He alarmed all the people of Down.

There was an Old Person of Cassel,
Whose Nose finished off in a Tassel;
    But they call'd out, " Oh well !—
    Don't it look like a bell ! "
Which perplexed that Old Person of Cassel.

There was an Old Man of Cashmere,
Whose movements were scroobious and queer;
    Being slender and tall,
    He looked over a wall,
And perceived two fat Ducks of Cashmere.

G

There was an Old Person of Hove,
Who frequented the depths of a grove;
　　Where he studied his Books,
　　With the Wrens and the Rooks,
That tranquil Old Person of Hove.

There was an Old Man of Spithead,
Who opened the window and said,—
    " Fil-jomble, fil-jumble,
    Fil-rumble-come-tumble ! "
That doubtful Old Man of Spithead.

There was an Old Man on the Border,
Who lived in the utmost disorder;
    He danced with the Cat,
    And made Tea in his Hat,
Which vexed all the folks on the Border.

There was an Old Person of Dundalk,
Who tried to teach Fishes to walk;
   When they tumbled down dead,
   He grew weary, and said,
"I had better go back to Dundalk!"

There was an Old Man of Dumbree,
Who taught little Owls to drink Tea;
    For he said, " To eat mice
    Is not proper or nice,"
That amiable Man of Dumbree.

There was an Old Person of Jodd,
Whose ways were perplexing and odd;
    She purchased a Whistle,
    And sate on a Thistle,
And squeaked to the people of Jodd.

There was an Old Person of Shoreham,
Whose habits were marked by decorum;
   He bought an Umbrella,
   And sate in the cellar,
Which pleased all the people of Shoreham.

There was an Old Man whose **remorse**,
Induced him to drink Caper Sauce ;
  For they said, " If mixed **up**
  With some cold claret-cup,
It will certainly soothe **your remorse** ! "

G*

There was an Old Person of Wilts,
Who constantly walked upon Stilts;
    He wreathed them with lilies
    And daffy-down-dillies,
That elegant Person of Wilts.

There was an Old Person of Pett,
Who was partly consumed by regret;
    He sate in a cart,
    And ate cold Apple Tart,
Which relieved that Old Person of Pett.

There was an Old Man of Port Grigor,
Whose actions were noted for vigour;
     He stood on his head,
     Till his waistcoat turned red,
That eclectic Old Man of Port Grigor.

There was an Old Person of Bar,
Who passed all her life in a Jar,
　　Which she painted pea-green,
　　To appear more serene,
That placid Old Person of Bar.

There was an Old Man of West Dumpet,
Who possessed a large Nose like a Trumpet;
　　When he blew it aloud,
　　It astonished the crowd,
And was heard through the whole of West Dumpet.

There was an Old Person of Grange,
Whose manners were scroobious and strange;
    He sailed to St. Blubb,
    In a Waterproof Tub,
That aquatic Old Person of Grange.

There was an Old Person of Nice,
Whose associates were usually Geese.
    They walked out together,
    In all sorts of weather,
That affable Person of Nice!

There was a Young Person of Kew,
Whose virtues and vices were few;
    But with blameable haste,
    She devoured some hot Paste,
Which destroyed that Young Person of Kew.

There was an Old Person of Sark,
Who made an unpleasant remark;
    But they said, "Don't you see
    What a brute you must be!
You obnoxious Old Person of Sark."

There was an Old Person of Filey,
Of whom his acquaintance spoke highly;
    He danced perfectly well
    To the sound of a bell,
And delighted the people of Filey.

There was an Old Man of El Hums,
Who lived upon nothing but Crumbs,
    Which he picked off the ground,
    With the other birds round,
In the roads and the lanes of El Hums.

There was an Old Man of Dunblane,
Who greatly resembled a Crane;
    But they said,—" Is it wrong,
    Since your legs are so long,
To request you won't stay in Dunblane?"

There was an Old Person of Hyde,
Who walked by the shore with his Bride,
    Till a Crab who came near,
    Fill'd their bosoms with fear,
And they said, " Would we'd never left Hyde ! "

There was an Old Person of Rimini,
Who said, " Gracious ! Goodness ! O Gimini ! "
    When they said, " Please be still ! "
    She ran down a Hill,
And was never more heard of at Rimini.

There was an Old Person of Cannes,
Who purchased three Fowls and a Fan;
    Those she placed on a Stool,
    And to make them feel cool
She constantly fanned them at Cannes.

There was an Old Person of Bude,
Whose deportment was vicious and crude;
    He wore a large Ruff
    Of pale straw-coloured stuff,
Which perplexed all the people of Bude.

There was an Old Person of Ickley,
Who could not abide to ride quickly;
    He rode to Karnak
    On a Tortoise's back,
That moony Old Person of Ickley.

There was an Old Man of Ancona,
Who found a small Dog with no Owner,
Which he took up and down
All the streets of the town;
That anxious Old Man of Ancona.

There was an Old Person of Barnes,
Whose Garments were covered with Darns;
 But they said, "Without doubt,
 You will soon wear them out,
You luminous Person of Barnes!"

There was an Old Person of Blythe,
Who cut up his Meat with a Scythe;
    When they said, " Well! I never! "—
    He cried, " Scythes for ever! "
That lively Old Person of Blythe.

There was an Old Person of Ealing,
Who was wholly devoid of good feeling;
    He drove a small Gig,
    With three Owls and a Pig,
Which distressed all the People of Ealing.

There was an Old Person of Bray,
Who sang through the whole of the Day
    To his Ducks and his Pigs,
    Whom he fed upon Figs,
That valuable Person of Bray.

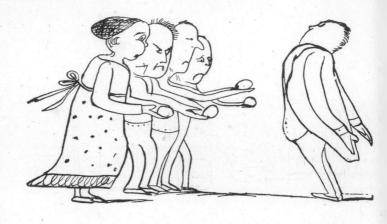

There was an Old Person of Bow,
Whom nobody happened to know;
 So they gave him some Soap,
 And said coldly, "We hope
You will go back directly to Bow!"

There was an Old Person in Gray,
Whose feelings were tinged with dismay;
    She purchased two Parrots
    And fed them with Carrots,
Which pleased that Old Person in Gray.

There was an Old Person of Crowle,
Who lived in the Nest of an Owl ;
    When they screamed in the Nest,
    He screamed out with the rest,
That depressing Old Person of Crowle.

There was an Old Person of Brigg,
Who purchased no end of a Wig ;
    So that only his Nose
    And the end of his Toes
Could be seen when he walked about Brigg.

There was a Young Lady of Greenwich,
Whose garments were border'd with Spinach;
　　But a large spotty Calf
　　Bit her Shawl quite in half,
Which alarmed that Young Lady of Greenwich.

There was an Old Person of Rye,
Who went up to town on a Fly;
    But they said, "If you cough,
    You are safe to fall off!
You abstemious Old Person of Rye!"

There was an Old Man of Messina,
Whose daughter was named Opsibeena;
 She wore a small Wig,
 And rode out on a Pig,
To the perfect delight of Messina.

There was a Young Lady whose Nose
Continually prospers and grows;
    When it grew out of sight,
    She exclaimed in a fright,
" Oh ! Farewell to the end of my Nose ! "

There was an Old Person of Sestri,
Who sate himself down in the vestry;
When they said, " You are wrong! "—
He merely said, " Bong! "
That repulsive Old Person of Sestri.

There was an Old Man in a Tree,
Whose Whiskers were lovely to see;
    But the Birds of the Air
    Pluck'd them perfectly bare,
To make themselves Nests in that Tree.

H*

There was a Young Lady of Corsica,
Who purchased a little brown Saucy-cur,
    Which she fed upon Ham
    And hot Raspberry Jam,
That expensive Young Lady of Corsica.

There was a Young Lady of Firle,
Whose Hair was addicted to curl;
    It curled up a Tree,
    And all over the Sea,
That expansive Young Lady of Firle.

There was an Old Lady of Winchelsea,
Who said, " If you Needle or Pin shall see,
   On the floor of my room,
    Sweep it up with the Broom ! "—
That exhaustive Old Lady of Winchelsea !

There was a Young Person whose History
Was always considered a Mystery;
    She sate in a Ditch,
    Although no one knew which,
And composed a small treatise on History.

There was an Old Man of Boulak,
Who sate on a Crocodile's back ;
    But they said, " Tow'rds the night
    He may probably bite,
Which might vex you, Old Man of Boulak ! "

There was an Old Man of Ibreem,
Who suddenly threaten'd to scream;
    But they said, " If you do,
    We will thump you quite blue,
You disgusting Old Man of Ibreem ! "

There was an Old Person of Stroud,
Who was horribly jammed in a crowd;
    Some she slew with a kick,
    Some she scrunched with a stick,
That impulsive Old Person of Stroud.

There was an Old Man of Thames Ditton,
Who called out for something to sit on:
  But they brought him a Hat,
  And said, " Sit upon that,
You abruptious Old Man of Thames Ditton ! "

There was an Old Person of Skye,
Who waltz'd with a Bluebottle Fly:
    They buzz'd a sweet tune,
    To the light of the moon,
And entranced all the people of Skye.

There was a Young Person of Ayr,
Whose Head was remarkably square:
    On the top, in fine weather,
    She wore a Gold Feather,
Which dazzled the people of Ayr.

There was an Old Person of Newry,
Whose manners were tinctured with fury;
    He tore all the Rugs,
    And broke all the Jugs,
Within twenty miles' distance of Newry.

There was a Young Lady of Poole,
Whose Soup was excessively cool;
    So she put it to boil
    By the aid of some Oil,
That ingenious Young Lady of Poole.

There was a Young Lady of Turkey,
Who wept when the weather was murky;
    When the day turned out fine,
    She ceased to repine,
That capricious Young Lady of Turkey.

There was an Old Man of Peru,
Who never knew what he should do;
    So he tore off his hair,
    And behaved like a bear,
That intrinsic Old Man of Peru.

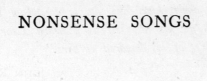

NONSENSE SONGS

THE OWL AND THE PUSSY-CAT.

I.

THE Owl and the Pussy-Cat went to sea
　　In a beautiful pea-green boat,
　　They took some honey, and plenty of
　　　money,
　　Wrapped up in a five-pound note.
The Owl looked up to the stars above,
　　And sang to a small guitar,
" O lovely Pussy ! O Pussy, my love,
　" What a beautiful Pussy you are,
　　　" You are,
　　　" You are !
　" What a beautiful Pussy you are ! "

II.

Pussy said to the Owl, " You elegant fowl !
 " How charmingly sweet you sing !
"O let us be married ! too long we have tarried
 " But what shall we do for a ring ? "
They sailed away for a year and a day,
 To the land where the Bong-tree grows,
And there in a wood a Piggy-wig stood,
 With a ring at the end of his nose,
 His nose,
 His nose,
 With a ring at the end of his nose.

III.

" Dear Pig, are you willing to sell for one shilling
 " Your ring ? " Said the Piggy, " I will."

So they took it away, and were married next day
  By the Turkey who lives on the hill.
They dinèd on mince, and slices of quince,[1]
  Which they ate with a runcible spoon;
And hand in hand, on the edge of the sand,
  They danced by the light of the moon,
      The moon,
      The moon,
  They danced by the light of the moon.

[1] Mr. Lear was delighted when I showed to him that this couple were reviving the old law of Solon, that the Athenian bride and bridegroom should eat a quince together at their wedding.—E. S.

THE DUCK AND THE KANGAROO.

I.

SAID the Duck to the Kangaroo,
  "Good gracious! how you hop!
  "Over the fields and the water too,
 "As if you never would stop!
"My life is a bore in this nasty pond,
"And I long to go out in the world beyond!
  "I wish I could hop like you!"
Said the Duck to the Kangaroo.

II.

"Please give me a ride on your back!'
  Said the Duck to the Kangaroo.
"I would sit quite still, and say nothing but
    'Quack,'
  "The whole of the long day through!

" And we'd go to the Dee, and the Jelly Bo Lee,
" Over the land, and over the sea ;—
  " Please take me a ride ! O do ! "
  Said the Duck to the Kangaroo.

III.

Said the Kangaroo to the Duck,
  " This requires some little reflection ;
" Perhaps on the whole it might bring me luck,
  " And there seems but one objection,
" Which is, if you'll let me speak so bold,
" Your feet are unpleasantly wet and cold,
  " And would probably give me the roo-
  " Matiz ! " said the Kangaroo.

IV.

Said the Duck, " As I sate on the rocks,

" I have thought over that completely,

" And I bought four pairs of worsted socks

" Which fit my web-feet neatly.

" And to keep out the cold I've bought a cloak,

" And every day a cigar I'll smoke,

" All to follow my own dear true

" Love of a Kangaroo ! "

V.

Said the Kangaroo, " I'm ready !

" All in the moonlight pale ;

" But to balance me well, dear Duck, sit steady !

" And quite at the end of my tail ! "

So away they went with a hop and a bound,

And they hopped the whole world three times
　　round;

　And who so happy,—O who,

　As the Duck and the Kangaroo?

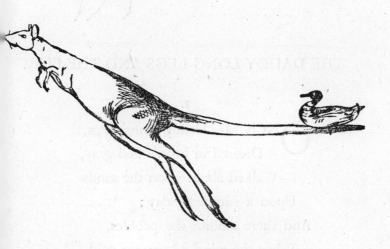

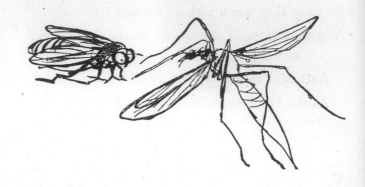

THE DADDY LONG-LEGS AND THE FLY.

I.

ONCE Mr. Daddy Long-Legs,
    Dressed in brown and gray,
  Walked about upon the sands
  Upon a summer's day;
And there among the pebbles,
    When the wind was rather cold,
He met with Mr. Floppy Fly,
    All dressed in blue and gold.
And as it was too soon to dine,
They drank some Periwinkle-wine,

And played an hour two, or more,
At battlecock and shuttledore.

II.

Said Mr. Daddy Long-Legs
   To Mr. Floppy Fly,
" Why do you never come to court?
   " I wish you'd tell me why.
" All gold and shine, in dress so fine,
   " You'd quite delight the court.
" Why do you never go at all?
   " I really think you *ought!*
" And if you went, you'd see such sights!
" Such rugs! and jugs! and candle-lights!
" And more than all, the King and Queen,
" One in red, and one in green!"

III.

" O Mr. Daddy Long-Legs,"
   Said Mr. Floppy Fly,

" It's true I never go to court,

　" And I will tell you why.

" If I had six long legs like yours,

　" At once I'd go to court !

" But oh ! I can't, because *my* legs

　" Are so extremely short.

" And I'm afraid the King and Queen

" (One in red, and one in green)

" Would say aloud, ' You are not fit,

" ' You Fly, to come to court a bit ! '

IV.

" O Mr. Daddy Long-Legs,"

　Said Mr. Floppy Fly,

" I wish you'd sing one little song !

　" One mumbian melody !

" You used to sing so awful well

　" In former days gone by,

" But now you never sing at all ;

　" I wish you'd tell me why :

" For if you would, the silvery sound
" Would please the shrimps and cockles round,
" And all the crabs would gladly come
" To hear you sing, ' Ah, Hum di Hum ! ' "

v.

Said Mr. Daddy Long-Legs,
  " I can never sing again !
" And if you wish, I'll tell you why,
  " Although it gives me pain.
" For years I could not hum a bit,
  " Or sing the smallest song ;
" And this the dreadful reason is,
  " My legs are grown too long !
" My six long legs, all here and there,
" Oppress my bosom with despair ;
" And if I stand, or lie, or sit,
" I cannot sing one single bit ! "

vi.

So Mr. Daddy Long-legs
  And Mr. Floppy Fly

Sat down in silence by the sea,
  And gazed upon the sky.
They said, " This is a dreadful thing !
  " The world has all gone wrong,
" Since one has legs too short by half,
  " The other much too long !
" One never more can go to court,
" Because his legs have grown too short ;
" The other cannot sing a song,
" Because his legs have grown too long ! "

VII.

Then Mr. Daddy Long-legs
  And Mr. Floppy Fly
Rushed downward to the foaming sea
  With one sponge-taneous cry ;
And there they found a little boat
  Whose sails were pink and gray ;
And off they sailed among the waves
  Far, and far away.

They sailed across the silent main
And reached the great Gromboolian plain;
And there they play for evermore
At battlecock and shuttledore.

THE JUMBLIES.

I.

THEY went to sea in a Sieve, they did,
   In a Sieve they went to sea:
   In spite of all their friends could say,
On a winter's morn, on a stormy day,
   In a Sieve they went to sea!
And when the Sieve turned round and round,
And every one cried, " You'll all be drowned ! "
They called aloud, " Our Sieve ain't big,
" But we don't care a button ! we don't care a fig !
   " In a Sieve we'll go to sea ! "

264

Far and few, far and few,

    Are the lands where the Jumblies live;

Their heads are green, and their hands are
    blue,

    And they went to sea in a Sieve.

II.

They sailed away in a Sieve, they did,

    In a Sieve they sailed so fast,

With only a beautiful pea-green veil

Tied with a riband by way of a sail,

    To a small tobacco-pipe mast;

And every one said, who saw them go,

" O won't they be soon upset, you know!

" For the sky is dark, and the voyage is long,

" And happen what may, it's extremely wrong

    " In a Sieve to sail so fast!"

    Far and few, far and few,

      Are the lands where the Jumblies live;

    Their heads are green, and their hands are
      blue,

      And they went to sea in a Sieve.

I*

III.

The water it soon came in, it did,

　　The water it soon came in ;

So to keep them dry, they wrapped their feet

In a pinky paper all folded neat,

　　And they fastened it down with a pin.

And they passed the night in a crockery-jar,

And each of them said, " How wise we are !

" Though the sky be dark, and the voyage be long,

" Yet we never can think we were rash or wrong,

　　" While round in our Sieve we spin ! "

　　　　Far and few, far and few,

　　　　　Are the lands where the Jumblies live ;

　　　　　Their heads are green, and their hands are blue,

　　　　　And they went to sea in a Sieve.

IV.

And all night long they sailed away ;

　　And when the sun went down,

They whistled and warbled a moony song

To the echoing sound of a coppery gong,

　　In the shade of the mountains brown.

" O Timballo ! How happy we are,
" When we live in a sieve and a crockery-jar.
" And all night long in the moonlight pale,
" We sail away with a pea-green sail,
 " In the shade of the mountains brown ! "
  Far and few, far and few,
   Are the lands where the Jumblies live ;
   Their heads are green, and their hands are
    blue
   And they went to sea in a Sieve.

v.

They sailed to the Western Sea, they did,
 To a land all covered with trees,
And they bought an Owl, and a useful Cart,
And a pound of Rice, and a Cranberry Tart,
 And a hive of silvery Bees.
And they bought a Pig, and some green Jackdaws,
And a lovely Monkey with lollipop paws,
And forty bottles of Ring-Bo-Ree,
 And no end of Stilton Cheese.

Far and few, far and few,
    Are the lands where the Jumblies live ;
Their heads are green, and their hands are blue,
    And they went to sea in a Sieve.

VI.

And in twenty years they all came back,
    In twenty years or more,
And every one said, " How tall they've grown !
" For they've been to the Lakes, and the Terrible
        Zone,
    " And the hills of the Chankly Bore ; "
And they drank their health, and gave them a feast
Of dumplings made of beautiful yeast ;
And every one said, " If we only live,
" We too will go to sea in a Sieve,—
    " To the hills of the Chankly Bore ! "
Far and few, far and few,
    Are the lands where the Jumblies live ;
Their heads are green, and their hands are blue,
    And they went to sea in a Sieve.

THE NUTCRACKERS AND THE SUGAR-TONGS.

I.

THE Nutcrackers sate by a plate on the table,
 The Sugar-tongs sate by a plate at his
 side;
And the Nutcrackers said, "Don't you wish we
 were able
 "Along the blue hills and green meadows to
 ride?
"Must we drag on this stupid existence for ever,
 "So idle and weary so full of remorse,—
"While every one else takes his pleasure and
 never
 "Seems happy unless he is riding a horse?

II.

"Don't you think we could ride without being
 instructed?
 "Without any saddle, or bridle, or spur?
"Our legs are so long, and so aptly constructed,
 "I'm sure that an accident could not occur.

269

" Let us all of a sudden hop down from the
  table,

  " And hustle downstairs, and each jump on a
    horse !

" Shall we try ? Shall we go ? Do you think we
  are able ? "

  The Sugar-tongs answered distinctly, " Of
    course ! "

III.

So down the long staircase they hopped in a
  minute,

  The Sugar-tongs snapped, and the Crackers
    said " crack ! "

The stable was open, the horses were in it ;

  Each took out a pony, and jumped on his back.

The Cat in a fright scrambled out of the doorway,

  The Mice tumbled out of a bundle of hay,

The brown and white Rats, and the black ones
  from Norway,

  Screamed out, " They are taking the horses
    away ! "

IV.

The whole of the household was filled with
    amazement,

  The Cups and the Saucers danced madly about,

The Plates and the Dishes looked out of the
    casement,

  The Saltcellar stood on his head with a shout,

The Spoons with a clatter looked out of the
    lattice,

  The Mustard-pot climbed up the Gooseberry
    Pies,

The Soup-ladle peeped through a heap of Veal
    Patties,

  And squeaked with a ladle-like scream of
    surprise.

V.

The Frying-pan said, " It's an awful delusion ! "

  The Tea-kettle hissed and grew black in the
    face ;

And they all rushed downstairs in the wildest
    confusion,

  To see the great Nutcracker-Sugar-tong race.

And out of the stable. with screamings and
    laughter,
  (Their ponies were cream-coloured, speckled
    with brown),
The Nutcrackers first, and the Sugar-tongs after,
  Rode all round the yard, and then all round
    the town.

VI.

They rode through the street, and they rode by
    the station,
  They galloped away to the beautiful shore;
In silence they rode, and " made no observation,"
  Save this : " We will never go back any
    more ! "
And still you might hear, till they rode out of
    hearing,
  The Sugar-tongs snap, and the Crackers say
    " crack ! "
Till far in the distance, their forms disappearing,
  They faded away.—And they never came back !

CALICO PIE.

I.

CALICO Pie,
   The Little Birds fly
Down to the calico tree,
Their wings were blue,
And they sang "Tilly-loo!"
Till away they flew,—
  And they never came back to me!
    They never came back!
    They never came back!
    They never came back to me!

II.

Calico Jam,
The little Fish swam
Over the syllabub sea,
He took off his hat,
To the Sole and the Sprat,
And the Willeby-wat,—

But he never came back to me !
He never came back !
He never came back !
He never came back to me !

III.

Calico Ban,
The little Mice ran,

To be ready in time for tea,
  Flippity flup,
  They drank it all up,
  And danced in the cup,—
But they never came back to me!
  They never came back!
  They never came back!
They never came back to me!

IV.

  Calico Drum,
  The Grasshoppers come,
The Butterfly, Beetle, and Bee,
  Over the ground,
  Around and round,
  With a hop and a bound,—

But they never came back!
They never came back!
They never came back!
They never came back to me!

MR. AND MRS. SPIKKY SPARROW.

I

ON a little piece of wood,
 Mr. Spikky Sparrow stood;
Mrs. Sparrow sate close by,
A-making of an insect pie,
For her little children five,
In the nest and all alive,
Singing with a cheerful smile
To amuse them all the while,
 Twikky wikky wikky wee,
 Wikky bikky twikky tee,
 Spikky bikky bee!

II.

Mrs. Spikky Sparrow said,
" Spikky, Darling ! in my head
" Many thoughts of trouble come,
" Like to flies upon a plum !
" All last night, among the trees,
" I heard you cough, I heard you sneeze ;
" And, thought I, it's come to that
" Because he does not wear a hat !
    " Chippy wippy sikky tee !
    " Bikky wikky tikky mee !
    " Spikky chippy wee !

III.

" Not that you are growing old,
" But the nights are growing cold.
" No one stays out all night long
" Without a hat : I'm sure it's wrong ! "
Mr. Spikky said, " How kind,
" Dear ! you are, to speak your mind !
" All your life I wish you luck !
" You are ! you are ! a lovely duck !

" Witchy witchy witchy wee !

" Twitchy witchy witchy bee !

" Tikky tikky tee !

IV.

" I was also sad, and, thinking,

" When one day I saw you winking,

" And I heard you sniffle-snuffle,

" And I saw your feathers ruffle ;

" To myself I sadly said,

" She's neuralgia in her head !

" That dear head has nothing on it !

" Ought she not to wear a bonnet ?

" Witchy kitchy kitchy wee !

" Spikky wikky mikky bee !

" Chippy wippy chee !

V.

" Let us both fly up to town !

" There I'll buy you such a gown !

" Which, completely in the fashion,

" You shall tie a sky-blue sash on.

" And a pair of slippers neat,
" To fit your darling little feet,
" So that you will look and feel
" Quite galloobious and genteel !
　" Jikky wikky bikky see !
　　" Chicky bikky wikky bee !
　　　" Twicky witchy wee ! "

VI.

So they both to London went,
Alighting on the Monument,
Whence they flew down swiftly—pop,
Into Moses' wholesale shop ;
There they bought a hat and bonnet,
And a gown with spots upon it,
A satin sash of Cloxam blue,
And a pair of slippers too.
　Zikky wikky mikky bee !
　　Witchy witchy mitchy kee !
　　　Sikky tikky wee !

VII.

Then when so completely drest,

Back they flew and reached their nest.

Their children cried, " O Ma and Pa!

" How truly beautiful you are!"

Said they, " We trust that cold or pain

" We shall never feel again!

" While, perched on tree, or house, or
steeple,

" We now shall look like other people.

" Witchy witchy witchy wee!

" Twikky mikky bikky bee!

" Zikky sikky tee!"

THE BROOM, THE SHOVEL, THE POKER,
AND THE TONGS.

I.

THE Broom and the Shovel, the Poker and
   Tongs,
 They all took a drive in the Park,
And they each sang a song, Ding-a-dong,
   Ding-a-dong,
 Before they went back in the dark.

Mr. Poker he sate quite upright in the coach,
  Mr. Tongs made a clatter and clash,
Miss Shovel was dressed all in black (with a
    brooch),
  Mrs. Broom was in blue (with a sash).
      Ding-a-dong! Ding-a-dong!
      And they all sang a song!

II.

" O Shovely so lovely ! " the Poker he sang,
  " You have perfectly conquered my heart !
" Ding-a-dong ! Ding-a-dong ! If you're pleased
    with my song
  " I will feed you with cold apple tart !
" When you scrape up the coals with a delicate
    sound,
  " You enrapture my life with delight !
" Your nose is so shiny ! your head is so round !
  " And your shape is so slender and bright !
    " Ding-a-dong! Ding-a-dong!
    " Ain't you pleased with my song ? "

III.

" Alas ! Mrs. Broom ! " sighed the Tongs in
his song,

" O is it because I'm so thin,

" And my legs are so long—Ding-a-dong !
Ding-a-dong !—

" That you don't care about me a pin ?

" Ah ! fairest of creatures, when sweeping the
room,

" Ah ! why don't you heed my complaint !

" Must you needs be so cruel, you beautiful
Broom,

" Because you are covered with paint ?

" Ding-a-dong ! Ding-a-dong !

" You are certainly wrong ! "

IV.

Mrs. Broom and Miss Shovel together they sang,

" What nonsense you're singing to-day ! "

Said the Shovel, " I'll certainly hit you a bang ! "

Said the Broom, " And I'll sweep you away ! "

So the Coachman drove homeward as fast as he
   could,
 Perceiving their anger with pain ;
But they put on the kettle, and little by little,
 They all became happy again.
   Ding-a-dong ! Ding-a-dong !
   There's an end of my song !

THE TABLE AND THE CHAIR.

I

SAID the Table to the Chair,
  " You can hardly be aware
  " How I suffer from the heat,
" And from chilblains on my feet !
" If we took a little walk,
" We might have a little talk !
" Pray let us take the air ! "
Said the Table to the Chair.

II.

Said the Chair unto the Table,
" Now you *know* we are not able !
" How foolishly you talk,
" When you know we *cannot* walk ! "
Said the Table with a sigh,
" It can do no harm to try ;
" I've as many legs as you,
" Why can't we walk on two ? "

III.

So they both went slowly down,
And walked about the town
With a cheerful bumpy sound,
As they toddled round and round.
And everybody cried,
As they hastened to their side,
" See ! the Table and the Chair
" Have come out to take the air ! "

IV.

But in going down an alley,
To a castle in the valley,
They completely lost their way,
And wandered all the day,
Till, to see them safely back.
They paid a Ducky-quack,
And a Beetle, and a Mouse,
Who took them to their house.

V.

Then they whispered to each other,
" O delightful little brother !
" What a lovely walk we've taken !
" Let us dine on Beans and Bacon ! "

So the Ducky and the leetle
Browny-Mousy and the Beetle
Dined, and danced upon their heads
Till they toddled to their beds.

THE DONG WITH A LUMINOUS NOSE.

WHEN awful darkness and silence reign
    Over the great Gromboolian plain,
  Through the long, long wintry nights;—
When the angry breakers roar
As they beat on the rocky shore;—
    When Storm-clouds brood on the towering
        heights
Of the Hills of the Chankly Bore:—

Then, through the vast and gloomy dark,
There moves what seems a fiery spark,
    A lonely spark with silvery rays

Piercing the coal-black night,—
A meteor strange and bright :—
Hither and thither the vision strays,
A single lurid light.

Slowly it wanders,—pauses,—creeps,—
Anon it sparkles,—flashes and leaps ;
And ever as onward it gleaming goes
A light on the Bong-tree stems it throws.
And those who watch at that midnight hour
From Hall or Terrace, or lofty Tower,
Cry, as the wild light passes along,—
      " The Dong !—the Dong !
   " The wandering Dong through the forest
         goes !
      " The Dong ! the Dong !
   " The Dong with a luminous Nose ! "

         Long years ago
      The Dong was happy and gay,
Till he fell in love with a Jumbly Girl
   Who came to those shores one day.

For the Jumblies came in a Sieve, they did,—
Landing at eve near the Zemmery Fidd
 Where the Oblong Oysters grow,
 And the rocks are smooth and gray.
And all the woods and the valleys rang
With the Chorus they daily and nightly sang,—
 " *Far and few, far and few,*
  Are the lands where the Jumblies live ;
  Their heads are green, and their hands are blue,
  And they went to sea in a Sieve."

Happily, happily passed those days !
 While the cheerful Jumblies staid ;
 They danced in circlets all night long,
 To the plaintive pipe of the lively Dong,
 In moonlight, shine, or shade.
For day and night he was always there
By the side of the Jumbly Girl so fair,
With her sky-blue hands, and her sea-green hair,
Till the morning came of that hateful day
When the Jumblies sailed in their Sieve away,

And the Dong was left on the cruel shore
Gazing—gazing for evermore,—
Ever keeping his weary eyes on
That pea-green sail on the far horizon,—
Singing the Jumbly Chorus still
As he sate all day on the grassy hill,—

> *" Far and few, far and few,*
> *Are the lands where the Jumblies live ;*
> *Their heads are green, and their hands are blue,*
> *And they went to sea in a Sieve."*

But when the sun was low in the West,
The Dong arose and said,—
" What little sense I once possessed
" Has quite gone out of my head ! "
And since that day he wanders still
By lake and forest, marsh and hill,
Singing—" O somewhere, in valley or plain
" Might I find my Jumbly Girl again !
" For ever I'll seek by lake and shore
" Till I find my Jumbly Girl once more ! "

Playing a pipe with silvery squeaks,
Since then his Jumbly Girl he seeks,
And because by night he could not see,
He gathered the bark of the Twangum Tree
    On the flowery plain that grows.
    And he wove him a wondrous Nose,—
  A Nose as strange as a Nose could be !
Of vast proportions and painted red,
And tied with cords to the back of his head.
    —In a hollow rounded space it ended
    With a luminous lamp within suspended
        All fenced about
        With a bandage stout
        To prevent the wind from blowing it
        out ;—
    And with holes all round to send the light,
    In gleaming rays on the dismal night.

And now each night, and all night long,
Over those plains still roams the Dong ;

And above the wail of the Chimp and Snipe
You may hear the squeak of his plaintive pipe
While ever he seeks, but seeks in vain
To meet with his Jumbly Girl again;
Lonely and wild—all night he goes,—
The Dong with a luminous Nose!
And all who watch at the midnight hour,
From Hall or Terrace, or lofty Tower,
Cry, as they trace the Meteor bright,
Moving along through the dreary night,—

    " This is the hour when forth he goes,

    " The Dong with a luminous Nose!

    " Yonder—over the plain he goes;

      " He goes!

      " He goes;

     " The Dong with a luminous Nose!"

THE TWO OLD BACHELORS.

TWO old Bachelors were living in one house;
    One caught a Muffin, the other caught
    a Mouse.

Said he who caught the Muffin to him who
    caught the Mouse,—

"This happens just in time! For we've nothing
    in the house,

"Save a tiny slice of lemon and a teaspoonful of
    honey,

"And what to do for dinner—since we haven't
    any money?

" And what can we expect if we haven't any
    dinner,

" But to lose our teeth and eyelashes and keep
    on growing thinner ? "

Said he who caught the Mouse to him who
    caught the Muffin,—

" We might cook this little Mouse, if we only
    had some Stuffin' !

" If we had but Sage and Onion we could do
    extremely well,

" But how to get that Stuffin' it is difficult to
    tell ! "—

Those two old Bachelors ran quickly to the town

And asked for Sage and Onion as they wandered
    up and down ;

They borrowed two large Onions, but no Sage
    was to be found

In the Shops, or in the Market, or in all the
    Gardens round.
    K*

But some one said,—" A hill there is, a little to
    the north,

" And to its purpledicular top a narrow way
    leads forth ;—

" And there among the rugged rocks abides an
    ancient Sage,—

" An earnest Man, who reads all day a most
    perplexing page.

" Climb up, and seize him by the toes !—all
    studious as he sits,—

" And pull him down,—and chop him into end-
    less little bits !

" Then mix him with your Onion (cut up likewise
    into Scraps),—

" When your Stuffin' will be ready—and very
    good : perhaps."

Those two old Bachelors without loss of time

The nearly purpledicular crags at once began to
    climb ;

And at the top, among the rocks, all seated in a
    nook,

They saw that Sage, a-reading of a most enormous
    book.

" You earnest Sage ! " aloud they cried, " your
    book you've read enough in !—

" We wish to chop you into bits to mix you into
    Stuffin' ! "

But that old Sage looked calmly up, and with
    his awful book,

At those two Bachelors' bald heads a certain aim
    he took ;—

And over crag and precipice they rolled pro-
    miscuous down,—

At once they rolled, and never stopped in lane
    or field or town,—

And when they reached their house, they found
    (besides their want of Stuffin'),

The Mouse had fled ;—and, previously, had
    eaten up the Muffin.

They left their home in silence by the once
    convivial door,

And from that hour those Bachelors were never
    heard of more.

THE PELICAN CHORUS.

KING and Queen of the Pelicans we;
  No other Birds so grand we see!
None but we have feet like fins!
With lovely leathery throats and chins!
    Ploffskin, Pluffskin, Pelican jee!
    We think no birds so happy as we!
    Plumpskin, Ploshkin, Pelican jill!
    We think so then, and we thought so still!

We live on the Nile. The Nile we love.
By night we sleep on the cliffs above.
By day we fish, and at eve we stand
On long bare islands of yellow sand.
And when the sun sinks slowly down
And the great rock walls grow dark and brown,
Where the purple river rolls fast and dim
And the ivory Ibis starlike skim,
Wing to wing we dance around,—
Stamping our feet with a flumpy sound,—
Opening our mouths as Pelicans ought,
And this is the song we nightly snort:

> Ploffskin, Pluffskin, Pelican jee!
> We think no Birds so happy as we!
> Plumpskin, Ploshkin, Pelican jill!
> We think so then, and we thought so still.

Last year came out our Daughter, Dell;
And all the Birds received her well.
To do her honour, a feast we made
For every bird that can swim or wade.

Herons and Gulls, and Cormorants black,
Cranes, and Flamingoes with scarlet back,
Plovers and Storks, and Geese in clouds,
Swans and Dilberry Ducks in crowds.
Thousands of Birds in wondrous flight !
They ate and drank and danced all night,
And echoing back from the rocks you heard
Multitude-echoes from Bird and Bird,—

> Ploffskin, Pluffskin, Pelican jee !
> We think no Birds so happy as we !
> Plumpskin, Ploshkin, Pelican jill !
> We think so then, and we thought so still !

Yes, they came ; and among the rest,
The King of the Cranes all grandly dressed.
Such a lovely tail ! Its feathers float
Between the ends of his blue dress-coat ;
With pea-green trowsers all so neat,
And a delicate frill to hide his feet,—
(For though no one speaks of it, every one knows,
He has got no webs between his toes !)

As soon as he saw our Daughter Dell,
In violent love that Crane King fell,—
On seeing her waddling form so fair,
With a wreath of shrimps in her short white hair,
And before the end of the next long day,
Our Dell had given her heart away;
For the King of the Cranes had won that heart,
With a Crocodile's egg and a large fish-tart.
She vowed to marry the King of the Cranes,
Leaving the Nile for stranger plains;
And away they flew in a gathering crowd
Of endless birds in a lengthening cloud.

    Ploffskin, Pluffskin, Pelican jee!
    We think no Birds so happy as we!
    Plumpskin, Ploshkin, Pelican jill!
    We think so then, and we thought so still!

And far away in the twilight sky,
We heard them singing a lessening cry,—
Farther and farther till out of sight,
And we stood alone in the silent night!

Often since, in the nights of June,
We sit on the sand and watch the moon ; —
She has gone to the great Gromboolian plain,
And we probably never shall meet again !
Oft, in the long still nights of June,
We sit on the rocks and watch the moon ;—
——She dwells by the streams of the Chankly
    Bore,
And we probably never shall see her more.

    Ploffskin, Pluffskin, Pelican jee !
    We think no Birds so happy as we !
    Plumpskin, Ploshkin, Pelican jill !
    We think so then, and we thought so still !

THE PELICANS

NOTE.—The air of this and the following Song by Edward Lear; the arrangement for the Piano by Professor Pomè, of San Remo, Italy.

THE PELICANS.

King and Queen of the Pel - i-cans we,

No oth-er birds so grand we see! None but we have

feet like fins, with love - ly lea- the - ry throats and chins.

Coro—più sostenuto.

Ploff - skin, Pluff - skin, Pe - li - can Jee! we think no birds so hap-py as we! Plump-skin, Ploff - skin, Pe - li - can Jill! We think so then, and we thought so still!

THE COURTSHIP OF THE YONGHY-
BONGHY-BÒ.

I.

ON the Coast of Coromandel
  Where the early pumpkins blow,
In the middle of the woods
  Lived the Yonghy-Bonghy-Bò.
Two old chairs, and half a candle,—
One old jug without a handle,—
    These were all his worldly goods:
    In the middle of the woods,
    These were all the worldly goods,

Of the Yonghy-Bonghy-Bò,
Of the Yonghy-Bonghy-Bò.

II.

Once, among the Bong-trees walking
 Where the early pumpkins blow,
  To a little heap of stones
 Came the Yonghy-Bonghy-Bò.
There he heard a Lady talking,
To some milk-white Hens of Dorking,—
   " 'Tis the Lady Jingly Jones !
   " On that little heap of stones
   " Sits the Lady Jingly Jones ! "
 Said the Yonghy-Bonghy-Bò,
 Said the Yonghy-Bonghy-Bò.

III.

" Lady Jingly ! Lady Jingly !
 " Sitting where the pumpkins blow,
  " Will you come and be my wife ? "
 Said the Yonghy-Bonghy-Bò.

"I am tired of living singly,—
"On this coast so wild and shingly,—
    "I'm a-weary of my life;
    "If you'll come and be my wife,
    "Quite serene would be my life!"—
Said the Yonghy-Bonghy-Bò,
Said the Yonghy-Bonghy-Bò.

IV.

"On this Coast of Coromandel,
    "Shrimps and watercresses grow,
        "Prawns are plentiful and cheap,"
Said the Yonghy-Bonghy-Bò.
"You shall have my chairs and candle,
"And my jug without a handle!—
    "Gaze upon the rolling deep
    ("Fish is plentiful and cheap);
    "As the sea, my love is deep!"
Said the Yonghy-Bonghy-Bò,
Said the Yonghy-Bonghy-Bò.

v.

Lady Jingly answered sadly,
  And her tears began to flow,—
    " Your proposal comes too late,
  " Mr. Yonghy-Bonghy-Bò !
" I would be your wife most gladly ! "
(Here she twirled her fingers madly)
    " But in England I've a mate !
    " Yes ! you've asked me far too late,
    " For in England I've a mate,
  " Mr. Yonghy-Bonghy-Bò !
  " Mr. Yonghy-Bonghy-Bò !

vi.

" Mr. Jones—(his name is Handel,—
  " Handel Jones, Esquire, & Co.)
    " Dorking fowls delights to send,
  " Mr. Yonghy-Bonghy-Bò !
" Keep, oh ! keep your chairs and candle,
" And your jug without a handle,—
    " I can merely be your friend !
    "—Should my Jones more Dorkings send,
    " I will give you three, my friend !

" Mr. Yonghy-Bonghy-Bò !
" Mr. Yonghy-Bonghy-Bò !

VII.

" Though you've such a tiny body,
    " And your head so large doth grow,—
        " Though your hat may blow away,
    " Mr. Yonghy-Bonghy-Bò !
" Though you're such a Hoddy Doddy—
" Yet I wish that I could modi-
        " fy the words I needs must say !
        " Will you please to go away ?
        " That is all I have to say—
" Mr. Yonghy-Bonghy-Bò !
" Mr. Yonghy-Bonghy-Bò !"

VIII.

Down the slippery slopes of Myrtle,
    Where the early pumpkins blow,
        To the calm and silent sea
    Fled the Yonghy-Bonghy-Bò.

There, beyond the Bay of Gurtle,
Lay a large and lively Turtle;—
   "You're the Cove," he said, "for me;
   "On your back beyond the sea,
   "Turtle, you shall carry me!"
Said the Yonghy-Bonghy-Bò,
Said the Yonghy-Bonghy-Bò.

IX.

Through the silent-roaring ocean
  Did the Turtle swiftly go;
   Holding fast upon his shell
  Rode the Yonghy-Bonghy-Bò.

With a sad primæval motion
Towards the sunset isles of Boshen
    Still the Turtle bore him well.
    Holding fast upon his shell,
     " Lady Jingly Jones, farewell ! "
Sang the Yonghy-Bonghy-Bò,
Sang the Yonghy-Bonghy-Bò.

X.

From the Coast of Coromandel,
    Did that Lady never go ;
     On that heap of stones she mourns
    For the Yonghy-Bonghy-Bò.
On that Coast of Coromandel,
In his jug without a handle,
     Still she weeps, and daily moans ;
     On that little heap of stones
     To her Dorking Hens she moans,
For the Yonghy-Bonghy-Bò,
For the Yonghy-Bonghy-Bò.

THE COURTSHIP OF
THE YONGHY-BONGHY-BÒ

THE YONGHY BONGHY BO.

CANTO.

PIANO.

On the coast of Co - ro -man-del, Where the

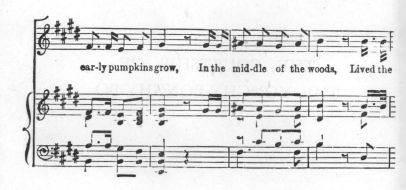

ear-ly pumpkins grow, In the mid-dle of the woods, Lived the

Yonghy Bonghy Bò; Two old chairs and half a candle, One old

jug without a han-dle; These were all his worldly goods, In the

mid-dle of the woods, These were all the world-ly goods, Of the

Yong - hy Bong - hy Bò, Of the Yong - hy Bong - hy Bò.

THE POBBLE WHO HAS NO TOES.

I.

THE Pobble who has no toes
    Had once as many as we;
When they said, "Some day you may lose
    them all;"—
    He replied,—"Fish fiddle de-dee!"
And his Aunt Jobiska made him drink,
Lavender water tinged with pink,
For she said, "The World in general knows
"There's nothing so good for a Pobble's toes!"

II.

The Pobble who has no toes,
   Swam across the Bristol Channel;
But before he set out he wrapped his nose
   In a piece of scarlet flannel.
For his Aunt Jobiska said, " No harm
" Can come to his toes if his nose is warm;
" And it's perfectly known that a Pobble's toes
" Are safe,—provided he minds his nose."

III.

The Pobble swam fast and well,
   And when boats or ships came near him
He tinkledy-binkledy-winkled a bell,
   So that all the world could hear him.
And all the Sailors and Admirals cried,
When they saw him nearing the further side,—
" He has gone to fish, for his Aunt Jobiska's
" Runcible Cat with crimson whiskers!"

IV.

But before he touched the shore,
　The shore of the Bristol Channel,
A sea-green Porpoise carried away
　His wrapper of scarlet flannel.
And when he came to observe his feet,
Formerly garnished with toes so neat,
His face at once became forlorn
On perceiving that all his toes were gone!

V.

And nobody ever knew
　From that dark day to the present,
Whoso had taken the Pobble's toes,
　In a manner so far from pleasant.
Whether the shrimps or crawfish gray,
Or crafty Mermaids stole them away—
Nobody knew; and nobody knows
How the Pobble was robbed of his twice five
　　　toes!

VI.

The Pobble who has no toes
   Was placed in a friendly Bark,
And they rowed him back, and carried him up,
   To his Aunt Jobiska's Park.
And she made him a feast at his earnest wish
Of eggs and buttercups fried with fish ;—
And she said,—" It's a fact the whole world
    knows,
" That Pobbles are happier without their toes."

THE NEW VESTMENTS.

THERE lived an old man in the Kingdom of
    Tess,
Who invented a purely original dress;
And when it was perfectly made and complete,
He opened the door, and walked into the street.

By way of a hat he'd a loaf of Brown Bread,
In the middle of which he inserted his head;—
His Shirt was made up of no end of dead Mice,
The warmth of whose skins was quite fluffy and
    nice;—
His Drawers were of Rabbit-skins;—so were his
    Shoes;—
His Stockings were skins,—but it is not known
    whose;—
His Waistcoat and Trowsers were made of
    Pork Chops;—
His Buttons were Jujubes, and Chocolate
    Drops;—
His Coat was all Pancakes with Jam for a border,
And a girdle of Biscuits to keep it in order;

And he wore over all, as a screen from bad
  weather,

A Cloak of green Cabbage-leaves stitched all
  together.

He had walked a short way, when he heard a
  great noise,

Of all sorts of Beasticles, Birdlings, and Boys ;—

And from every long street and dark lane in the
  town

Beasts, Birdles, and Boys in a tumult rushed down.

Two Cows and a Calf ate his Cabbage-leaf
  Cloak ;—

Four Apes seized his Girdle, which vanished like
  smoke ;—

Three Kids ate up half of his Pancaky Coat,—

And the tails were devoured by an ancient He
  Goat ;—

An army of Dogs in a twinkling tore *up* his

Pork Waistcoat and Trowsers to give to their
  Puppies ;—

And while they were growling, and mumbling
  the Chops,

Ten Boys prigged the Jujubes and Chocolate
  Drops.—

He tried to run back to his house, but in vain,

For scores of fat Pigs came again and again ;—

They rushed out of stables and hovels and doors,—

They tore off his stockings, his shoes, and his drawers ;—

And now from the housetops with screechings descend,

Striped, spotted, white, black, and gray cats without end,

They jumped on his shoulders and knocked off his hat,—

When Crows, Ducks and Hens made a mince-meat of that ;—

They speedily flew at his sleeves in a trice,

And utterly tore up his Shirt of dead Mice ;—

They swallowed the last of his Shirt with a squall,—

Whereon he ran home with no clothes on at all.

And he said to himself as he bolted the door,

" I will not wear a similar dress any more,

" Any more, any more, any more, never more ! "

MR. AND MRS. DISCOBBOLOS.

FIRST PART.

I.

MR. AND MRS. DISCOBBOLOS
Climbed to the top of a wall,
And they sate to watch the sunset sky
And to hear the Nupiter Piffkin cry
And the Biscuit Buffalo call.
They took up a roll and some Camomile tea,
And both were as happy as happy could be—
Till Mrs. Discobbolos said,—
"Oh! W! X! Y! Z!
"It has just come into my head—
"Suppose we should happen to fall!!!!!
"Darling Mr. Discobbolos?

II.

"Suppose we should fall down flumpetty
"Just like two pieces of stone!
"On to the thorns,—or into the moat!
"What would become of your new green
coat?
"And might you not break a bone?

" It never occurred to me before—

" That perhaps we shall never go down any
            more ! "

            And Mrs. Discobbolos said—

            " Oh ! W ! X ! Y ! Z !

            " What put it into your head

" To climb up this wall ?—my own

                        " Darling Mr. Discobbolos ? "

III.

Mr. Discobbolos answered,—

            " At first it gave me pain,—

            " And I felt my ears turn perfectly pink

            " When your exclamation made me think

            " We might never get down again !

" But now I believe it is wiser far

" To remain for ever just where we are."—

            And Mr. Discobbolos said,

            " Oh ! W ! X ! Y ! Z !

            " It has just come into my head—

            " ——We shall never go down again—

                        " Dearest Mrs. Discobbolos ! "

IV.

So Mr. and Mrs. Discobbolos
   Stood up, and began to sing,
  " Far away from hurry and strife
  " Here we will pass the rest of life,
    " Ding a dong, ding dong, ding !
" We want no knives nor forks nor chairs,
" No tables nor carpets nor household cares,
     " From worry of life we've fled—
     " Oh ! W ! X ! Y ! Z !
     " There is no more trouble ahead
    " Sorrow or any such thing—
       " For Mr. and Mrs. Discobbolos ! "

MR. AND MRS. DISCOBBOLOS.

SECOND PART.

I.

MR. AND MRS. DISCOBBOLOS
Lived on the top of the wall,
For twenty years, a month and a day,
Till their hair had grown all pearly gray,
And their teeth began to fall.
They never were ill, or at all dejected,
By all admired, and by some respected,
Till Mrs. Discobbolos said,
" Oh! W! X! Y! Z!
" It has just come into my head,
" We have no more room at all—

" Darling Mr. Discobbolos!

328

II.

" Look at our six fine boys !

" And our six sweet girls so fair !

" Upon this wall they have all been born,

" And not one of the twelve has happened to fall

" Through my maternal care !

" Surely they should not pass their lives

" Without any chance of husbands or wives ! "

And Mrs. Discobbolos said,

" Oh ! W ! X ! Y ! Z !

" Did it never come into your head

" That our lives must be lived elsewhere,

" Dearest Mr. Discobbolos ?

III.

" They have never been at a ball,

" Nor have even seen a bazaar !

" Nor have heard folks say in a tone all hearty,

" What loves of girls (at a garden party)

Those Misses Discobbolos are ! '

L*

" Morning and night it drives me wild
" To think of the fate of each darling child ! "
   But Mr. Discobbolos said,
    " Oh ! W ! X ! Y ! Z !
     " What has come to your fiddledum head !
  " What a runcible goose you are !
      " Octopod Mrs. Discobbolos ! "

IV.

Suddenly Mr. Discobbolos
  Slid from the top of the wall ;
  And beneath it he dug a dreadful trench,
  And filled it with dynamite, gunpowder gench,
   And aloud he began to call—
" Let the wild bee sing,
" And the blue bird hum !
" For the end of your lives has certainly come ! "
   And Mrs. Discobbolos said,
    " Oh ! W ! X ! Y ! Z !
     " We shall presently all be dead,
" On this ancient runcible wall,
      " Terrible Mr. Discobbolos ! "

v.

Pensively, Mr. Discobbolos
   Sat with his back to the wall ;
  He lighted a match, and fired the train,
  And the mortified mountain echoed again
   To the sound of an awful fall !
And all the Discobbolos family flew
In thousands of bits to the sky so blue,
   And no one was left to have said,
   " Oh ! W ! X ! Y ! Z !
   " Has it come into anyone's head
  " That the end has happened to all
   " Of the whole of the Clan Discobbolos ? "

THE QUANGLE WANGLE'S HAT.

I.

ON the top of the Crumpetty Tree
    The Quangle Wangle sat,
But his face you could not see,
    On account of his Beaver Hat.
For his Hat was a hundred and two feet wide,
With ribbons and bibbons on every side
And bells, and buttons, and loops, and lace,
So that nobody ever could see the face
    Of the Quangle Wangle Quee.

332

II.

The Quangle Wangle said
   To himself on the Crumpetty Tree,—
" Jam ; and jelly ; and bread ;
   " Are the best of food for me !
" But the longer I live on this Crumpetty Tree,
" The plainer than ever it seems to me
" That very few people come this way,
" And that life on the whole is far from gay ! "
     Said the Quangle Wangle Quee.

III.

But there came to the Crumpetty Tree,
   Mr. and Mrs. Canary ;
And they said,—" Did ever you see
   " Any spot so charmingly airy ?
" May we build a nest on your lovely Hat ?
" Mr. Quangle Wangle, grant us that !
" O please let us come and build a nest
" Of whatever material suits you best,
     " Mr. Quangle Wangle Quee ! "

IV.

And besides, to the Crumpetty Tree
   Came the Stork, the Duck, and the Owl;
The Snail and the Bumble-Bee,
   The Frog, and the Fimble Fowl;
(The Fimble Fowl, with a Corkscrew leg);
And all of them said,—" We humbly beg,
" We may build our homes on your lovely Hat,—
" Mr. Quangle Wangle, grant us that!
     " Mr. Quangle Wangle Quee!"

V.

And the Golden Grouse came there,
   And the Pobble who has no toes,—
And the small Olympian bear,—
   And the Dong with a luminous nose.
And the Blue Baboon, who played the flute,—
And the Orient Calf from the Land of Tute,—
And the Attery Squash, and the Bisky Bat,—
All came and built on the lovely Hat
    Of the Quangle Wangle Quee.

VI.

And the Quangle Wangle said
  To himself on the Crumpetty Tree,—
" When all these creatures move
  " What a wonderful noise there'll be ! "
And at night by the light of the Mulberry moon
They danced to the Flute of the Blue Baboon,
On the broad green leaves of the Crumpetty Tree,
And all were as happy as happy could be,
  With the Quangle Wangle Quee.

THE CUMMERBUND.

AN INDIAN POEM.

I.

SHE sate upon her Dobie,[1]
  To watch the Evening Star,
And all the Punkahs[2] as they passed
  Cried, " My ! how fair you are ! "
Around her bower, with quivering leaves
  The tall Kamsamahs[3] grew,
And Kitmutgars[4] in wild festoons
  Hung down from Tchokis[5] blue.

II.

Below her home the river rolled
  With soft meloobious sound,
Where golden-finned Chuprassies[6] swam,
  In myriads circling round.

---

[1] Washerman.   [2] Fan.   [3] Butler.   [4] Waiter at Table.
   [5] Police or post station.   [6] Office messenger.

Above, on tallest trees remote,
  Green Ayahs perched alone,
And all night long the Mussak[1] moan'd
  Its melancholy tone.

III.

And where the purple Nullahs[2] threw
  Their branches far and wide,—
And silvery Goreewallahs[3] flew
  In silence, side by side,—
The little Bheesties'[4] twittering cry
  Rose on the fragrant air,
And oft the angry Jampan[5] howled
  Deep in his hateful lair.

IV.

She sate upon her Dobie,—
  She heard the Nimmak[6] hum,—
When all at once a cry arose:
  " The Cummerbund[7] is come ! "

---

[1] Water skin. [2] Watercourse. [3] Groom. [4] Water-carrier.
  [5] Sedan chair. [6] Salt. [7] Waist-sash.

In vain she fled ;—with open jaws
    The angry monster followed,
And so, (before assistance came),
    That Lady Fair was swollowed.

v.

They sought in vain for even a bone
    Respectfully to bury,—
They said, " Hers was a dreadful fate ! "
    (And Echo answered " Very.")
They nailed her Dobie to the wall,
    Where last her form was seen,
And underneath they wrote these words,
    In yellow, blue, and green :—

Beware, ye Fair ! Ye Fair, beware !
    Nor sit out late at night,—
Lest horrid Cummerbunds should come,
    And swollow you outright.

THE AKOND OF SWAT.

WHO or why, or which, or *what*,
        Is the Akond of SWAT?

Is he tall or short, or dark or fair?
Does he sit on a stool or a sofa or chair,
       or SQUAT,
        The Akond of Swat?

Is he wise or foolish, young or old?
Does he drink his soup and his coffee cold,
       or HOT,
        The Akond of Swat?

Does he sing or whistle, jabber or talk,
And when riding abroad does he gallop or walk,
       or TROT,
        The Akond of Swat?

Does he wear a turban, a fez, or a hat?
Does he sleep on a mattress, a bed, or a mat,
       or a COT,
        The Akond of Swat?

When he writes a copy in round-hand size,
Does he cross his T's and finish his I's
                    with a DOT,
                        The Akond of Swat?

Can he write a letter concisely clear
Without a speck or a smudge or smear
                    or BLOT,
                        The Akond of Swat!

Do his people like him extremely well?
Or do they, whenever they can, rebel,
                    or PLOT,
                        At the Akond of Swat?

If he catches them then, either old or young,
Does he have them chopped in pieces or hung,
                    or SHOT,
                        The Akond of Swat?

Do his people prig in the lanes or park?
Or even at times, when days are dark,
                    GAROTTE?
                        O the Akond of Swat!

Does he study the wants of his own dominion?
Or doesn't he care for public opinion

a JOT,

The Akond of Swat?

To amuse his mind do his people show him
Pictures, or any one's last new poem,

or WHAT,

For the Akond of Swat?

At night if he suddenly screams and wakes,
Do they bring him only a few small cakes,

or a LOT,

For the Akond of Swat?

Does he live on turnips, tea, or tripe?
Does he like his shawl to be marked with a stripe,

or a DOT,

The Akond of Swat?

Does he like to lie on his back in a boat
Like the lady who lived in that isle remote,

SHALLOTT,

The Akond of Swat?

Is he quiet, or always making a fuss?
Is his steward a Swiss or a Swede or a Russ,
                    or a SCOT,
                    The Akond of Swat?

Does he like to sit by the calm blue wave?
Or to sleep and snore in a dark green cave,
                    or a GROTT,
                    The Akond of Swat?

Does he drink small beer from a silver jug?
Or a bowl? or a glass? or a cup? or a mug?
                    or a POT,
                    The Akond of Swat?

Does he beat his wife with a gold-topped pipe,
When she lets the gooseberries grow too ripe,
                    or ROT,
                    The Akond of Swat?

Does he wear a white tie when he dines with
     friends,
And tie it neat in a bow with ends,
                    or a KNOT,
                    The Akond of Swat?

Does he like new cream, and hate mince-pies?

When he looks at the sun does he wink his eyes,

or NOT,

The Akond of Swat?

Does he teach his subjects to roast and bake?

Does he sail about on an inland lake,

in a YACHT,

The Akond of Swat?

Some one, or nobody, knows, I wot,

Who or which or why or what

Is the Akond of Swat!

NOTE.—For the existence of this potentate see Indian newspapers, *passim.* The proper way to read the verses is to make an immense emphasis on the monosyllabic rhymes, which indeed ought to be shouted out by a chorus.

INCIDENTS IN THE LIFE OF MY UNCLE ARLY.

I.

O MY AGÈD UNCLE ARLY!
Sitting on a heap of Barley
Thro' the silent hours of night,—
Close beside a leafy thicket:—
On his nose there was a Cricket,—
In his hat a Railway-Ticket;—
(But his shoes were far too tight).

II.

Long ago, in youth, he squander'd
All his goods away, and wander'd
To the Tiniskoop-hills afar.

344

There on golden sunsets blazing,
Every evening found him gazing,—
Singing,—" Orb ! you're quite amazing !
" How I wonder what you are ! "

III.

Like the ancient Medes and Persians,
Always by his own exertions
He subsisted on those hills ;—
Whiles,—by teaching children spelling,—
Or at times by merely yelling,—
Or at intervals by selling
" Propter's Nicodemus Pills."

IV.

Later, in his morning rambles
He perceived the moving brambles
Something square and white disclose ;—
'Twas a First-class Railway-Ticket ;
But, on stooping down to pick it
Off the ground,—a pea-green Cricket
Settled on my uncle's Nose.

V.

Never—never more,—oh ! never,
Did that Cricket leave him ever,—
    Dawn or evening, day or night ;—
Clinging as a constant treasure,—
Chirping with a cheerious measure,—
Wholly to my uncle's pleasure,—
    (Though his shoes were far too tight).

VI.

So for three-and-forty winters,
Till his shoes were worn to splinters,
    All those hills he wander'd o'er,—
Sometimes silent ;—sometimes yelling ;—
Till he came to Borley-Melling,
Near his old ancestral dwelling ;—
    (But his shoes were far too tight).

VII.

On a little heap of Barley
Died my agèd uncle Arly,

And they buried him one night ;—
Close beside the leafy thicket ;—
There,—his hat and Railway-Ticket ;—
There,—his ever-faithful Cricket ;—
(But his shoes were far too tight).

ECLOGUE.

COMPOSED AT CANNES, DECEMBER 9TH, 1867.

[*Interlocutors*—MR. LEAR AND MR. AND MRS. SYMONDS.]

Edwardus.—

WHAT makes you look so black, so glum, so cross?

Is it neuralgia, headache, or remorse?

Johannes.—

What makes you look as cross, or even more so?

Less like a man than is a broken Torso?

E.—What if my life is odious, should I grin?

If you are savage, need I care a pin?

J.—And if I suffer, am I then an owl?

May I not frown and grind my teeth and growl?

E.—Of course you may; but may not I growl too?

May I not frown and grind my teeth like you?

J.—See Catherine comes ! To her, to her,

Let each his several miseries refer ;

She shall decide whose woes are least or worst,

And which, as growler, shall rank last or first.

Catherine.—

Proceed to growl, in silence I'll attend,

And hear your foolish growlings to the end ;

And when they're done, I shall correctly judge

Which of your griefs are real or only fudge.

Begin, let each his mournful voice prepare,

(And, pray, however angry, do not swear !)

J.—We came abroad for warmth, and find sharp cold !

Cannes is an imposition, and we're sold.

E.—Why did I leave my native land, to find

Sharp hailstones, snow, and most disgusting wind ?

J.—What boots it that we orange trees or lemons
    see,

    If we must suffer from *such* vile inclemency ?

E.—Why did I take the lodgings I have got,

    Where all I don't want is :—all I want not ?

J.—Last week I called aloud, O ! O ! O ! O !

    The ground is wholly overspread with
    snow !

    Is that at any rate a theme for mirth

    Which makes a sugar-cake of all the earth ?

E.—Why must I sneeze and snuffle, groan and
    cough,

    If my hat's on my head, or if it's off ?

    Why must I sink all poetry in this prose,

    The everlasting blowing of my nose ?

J.—When I walk out the mud my footsteps
    clogs,

    Besides, I suffer from attacks of dogs.

E.—Me a vast awful bulldog, black and brown,
Completely terrified when near the town ;
As calves, perceiving butchers, trembling reel,
So did *my* calves the approaching monster feel.

J.—Already from two rooms we're driven away,
Because the beastly chimneys smoke all day :
Is this a trifle, say ? Is this a joke ?
That we, like hams, should be becooked in smoke ?

E.—Say ! what avails it that my servant speaks
Italian, English, Arabic, and Greek,
Besides Albanian : if he don't speak French,
How can he ask for salt, or shrimps, or tench ?

J.—When on the foolish hearth fresh wood I place,
It whistles, sings, and squeaks, before my face :

And if it does unless the fire burns bright,

And if it does, yet squeaks, how can I write?

E.—Alas! I needs must go and call on swells,

That they may say, " Pray draw me the Estrelles."

On one I went last week to leave a card,

The swell was out—the servant eyed me hard :

" This chap's a thief disguised," his face expressed :

If I go there again, may I be blest !

J.—Why must I suffer in this wind and gloom ?

Roomattics in a vile cold attic room ?

E.—Swells drive about the road with haste and fury,

As Jehu drove about all over Jewry.

Just now, while walking slowly, I was all but

Run over by the Lady Emma Talbot,

Whom not long since a lovely babe I knew,

With eyes and cap-ribbons of perfect blue.

J.—Downstairs and upstairs, every blessed minute,

There's each room with pianofortes in it.

How can I write with noises such as those?

And, being always discomposed, compose?

E.—Seven Germans through my garden lately strayed,

And all on instruments of torture played;

They blew, they screamed, they yelled: how can I paint

Unless my room is quiet, which it ain't?

J.—How can I study if a hundred flies

Each moment blunder into both my eyes?

E.—How can I draw with green or blue or red,

If flies and beetles vex my old bald head?

J.—How can I translate German Metaphys-

-Ics, if mosquitoes round my forehead whizz?

M

E.—I've bought some bacon, (though it's much
    too fat,)

    But round the house there prowls a hideous
    cat :

    Once should I see my bacon in her mouth,

    What care I if my rooms look north or
    south ?

J.—Pain from a pane in one cracked window
    comes,

    Which sings and whistles, buzzes, shrieks
    and hums ;

    In vain amain with pain the pane with this
    chord

    I fain would strain to stop the beastly
    *dis*cord ?

E.—If rain and wind and snow and such like ills

    Continue here, how shall I pay my bills ?

    For who through cold and slush and rain
    will come

    To see my drawings and to purchase some ?

    And if they don't, what destiny is mine ?

    How can I ever get to Palestine ?

J.—The blinding sun strikes through the olive trees,

When I walk out, and always makes me sneeze.

E.—Next door, if all night long the moon is shining,

There sits a dog, who wakes me up with whining.

Cath.—Forbear! You both are bores, you've growled enough:

No longer will I listen to such stuff!

All men have nuisances and bores to afflict 'um:

Hark then, and bow to my official dictum!

For you, Johannes, there is most excuse,

(Some interruptions are the very deuce,)

You're younger than the other cove, who surely

Might have some sense—besides, you're somewhat poorly.

This therefore is my sentence, that you nurse
The Baby for seven hours, and nothing
worse.

For you, Edwardus, I shall say no more
Than that your griefs are fudge, yourself a
bore :
Return at once to cold, stewed, minced,
hashed mutton—
To wristbands ever guiltless of a button—
To raging winds and sea, (where don't you
wish
Your luck may ever let you catch one
fish ?)—
To make large drawings nobody will buy—
To paint oil pictures which will never dry—
To write new books which nobody will
read—
To drink weak tea, on tough old pigs to
feed—
Till spring-time brings the birds and leaves
and flowers,
And time restores a world of happier hours.

NONSENSE STORIES

AND

ALPHABETS

THE STORY OF THE FOUR LITTLE CHILDREN WHO WENT ROUND THE WORLD

ONCE upon a time, a long while ago, there were four little people whose names were

VIOLET,   SLINGSBY,   GUY, and LIONEL;

and they all thought they should like to see the world. So they bought a large boat to sail quite round the world by sea, and then they were to come back on the other side by land. The boat was painted blue with green spots, and the sail was yellow with red stripes; and when they set off, they only took a small Cat to steer and look after the boat, besides an elderly Quangle-Wangle, who had to cook the dinner and make the tea; for which purposes they took a large kettle.

For the first ten days they sailed on beautifully, and found plenty to eat, as there were lots of fish, and they had only to take them out of the sea with a long spoon, when the Quangle-Wangle instantly cooked them, and the Pussy-Cat was fed with the bones, with which she expressed herself pleased on the whole, so that all the party were very happy.

During the day-time, Violet chiefly occupied herself in putting salt-water into a churn, while her three brothers churned it violently, in the hope that it would turn into butter, which it seldom, if ever did; and in the evening they all retired into the Tea-kettle, where they all managed to sleep very comfortably, while Pussy and the Quangle-Wangle managed the boat.

M*

After a time they saw some land at a distance;
and when they came to it, they found it was an

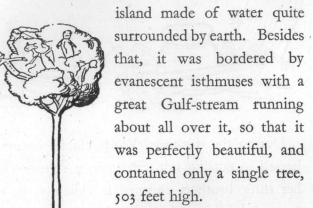

island made of water quite
surrounded by earth. Besides
that, it was bordered by
evanescent isthmuses with a
great Gulf-stream running
about all over it, so that it
was perfectly beautiful, and
contained only a single tree,
503 feet high.

When they had landed,
they walked about, but found
to their great surprise that
the island was quite full of
veal-cutlets and chocolate-
drops, and nothing else. So
they all climbed up the single
high tree to discover, if
possible, if there were any
people; but having remained on the top of the
tree for a week, and not seeing anybody,

they naturally concluded that there were no inhabitants, and accordingly when they came down they loaded the boat with two thousand veal-cutlets and a million of chocolate drops, and these afforded them sustenance for more than a month, during which time they pursued their voyage with the utmost delight and apathy.

After this they came to a shore where there were no less than sixty-five great red parrots with blue tails, sitting on a rail all of a row, and all fast asleep. And I am sorry to say that the Pussy-Cat and the Quangle-Wangle crept softly and bit off the tail-feathers of all the sixty-five parrots, for which Violet reproved them both severely.

Notwithstanding which, she proceeded to insert all the feathers, two hundred and sixty in

number, in her bonnet, thereby causing it to have a lovely and glittering appearance, highly prepossessing and efficacious.

The next thing that happened to them was in a narrow part of the sea, which was so entirely

full of fishes that the boat could go no further; so they remained there about six weeks, till they had eaten nearly all the fishes, which were Soles, and all ready-cooked and covered with shrimp sauce, so that there was no trouble whatever. And as the few fishes who remained uneaten complained of the cold, as well as of the difficulty they had in getting any sleep on account of the extreme noise made by the Arctic Bears and the Tropical Turnspits, which frequented the neighbourhood in great numbers, Violet most amiably knitted a small woollen

frock for several of the fishes, and Slingsby administered some opium drops to them, through which kindness they became quite warm and slept soundly.

Then they came to a country which was wholly covered with immense Orange-trees of a vast size, and quite full of fruit. So they all landed, taking with them the Tea-kettle, intending to gather some of the Oranges and place them in it. But while they were busy about this, a most dreadfully high wind rose, and blew out most of the parrot-tail feathers from Violet's bonnet. That, however, was nothing compared with the calamity of the Oranges falling down on their heads by millions and millions, which thumped and bumped and bumped and thumped them all so seriously that they were obliged to run as hard as they could for their lives, besides that the sound of the Oranges rattling on the Tea-kettle was of the most fearful and amazing nature.

Nevertheless they got safely to the boat, although considerably vexed and hurt; and the

Quangle-Wangle's right foot was so knocked about that he had to sit with his head in his slipper for at least a week.

This event made them all for a time rather melancholy, and perhaps they might never have become less so, had not Lionel, with a most praiseworthy devotion and perseverance, continued to stand on one leg and whistle to them in a loud and lively manner, which diverted the whole party so extremely, that they gradually recovered their spirits, and agreed that whenever they should reach home they would subscribe towards a testimony to Lionel, entirely made of

Gingerbread and Raspberries, as an earnest token of their sincere and grateful infection.

After sailing on calmly for several more days, they came to another country, where they were

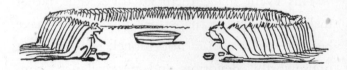

much pleased and surprised to see a countless multitude of white Mice with red eyes, all sitting in a great circle, slowly eating Custard Pudding with the most satisfactory and polite demeanour.

And as the four Travellers were rather hungry, being tired of eating nothing but Soles and

Oranges for so long a period, they held a council
as to the propriety of asking the Mice for some
of their pudding in a humble and affecting
manner, by which they could hardly be other-
wise than gratified. It was agreed therefore that
Guy should go and ask the Mice, which he
immediately did ; and the result was that they
gave a Walnut-shell only half full of Custard
diluted with water. Now, this displeased Guy,
who said, " Out of such a lot of Pudding as you
have got, I must say you might have spared a
somewhat larger quantity ! " But no sooner
had he finished speaking than all the Mice turned
round at once, and sneezed at him in an appalling

and vindictive manner (and it is impossible to
imagine a more scroobious and unpleasant sound
than that caused by the simultaneous sneezing of
many millions of angry Mice), so that Guy

rushed back to the boat, having first shied his cap into the middle of the Custard Pudding, by which means he completely spoiled the Mice's dinner.

By-and-by the Four Children came to a country where there were no houses, but only an incredibly innumerable number of large bottles without corks, and of a dazzling and sweetly susceptible blue colour. Each of these blue bottles contained a Blue-Bottle-Fly, and all these interesting animals live continually together in the most copious and rural harmony, nor perhaps in many parts of the world is such perfect and abject happiness to be found. Violet, and Slingsby, and Guy, and Lionel, were greatly struck with this singular and instructive settlement, and having previously asked permission of the Blue-Bottle-Flies (which was most courteously granted), the boat was drawn up to the shore, and they proceeded to make tea in front of the bottles ; but as they had no tea-leaves, they merely placed some pebbles in the hot water,

and the Quangle-Wangle played some tunes over it on an Accordion, by which of course tea was made directly, and of the very best quality.

The Four Children then entered into conversation with the Blue-Bottle-Flies, who discoursed in a placid and genteel manner, though with a slightly buzzing accent, chiefly owing to the fact that they each held a small clothes-brush between their teeth, which naturally occasioned a fizzy extraneous utterance.

"Why," said Violet, "would you kindly inform us, do you reside in bottles? and if in bottles at all, why not rather in green or purple, or indeed in yellow bottles?"

To which questions a very aged Blue-Bottle-Fly answered, "We found the bottles here all ready to live in, that is to say, our great-great-

great-great-great-grandfathers did, so we occupied them at once. And when the winter comes on, we turn the bottles upside-down, and consequently rarely feel the cold at all, and you know very well that this could not be the case with bottles of any other colour than blue."

" Of course it could not," said Slingsby; " but if we may take the liberty of inquiring, on what do you chiefly subsist ? "

" Mainly on Oyster-patties," said the Blue-Bottle-Fly, " and when these are scarce, on Raspberry Vinegar and Russian leather boiled down to a jelly."

" How delicious ! " said Guy.

To which Lionel added, " Huzz ! " and all the Blue-Bottle-Flies said " Buzz ! "

At this time, an elderly Fly said it was the hour for the Evening-song to be sung; and on a signal being given all the Blue-Bottle-Flies began to buzz at once in a sumptuous and sonorous manner, the melodious and mucilaginous sounds echoing all over the waters, and resounding across the tumultuous tops of the transitory Titmice upon the intervening and verdant mountains, with a serene and sickly suavity only known to the truly virtuous. The Moon was shining slobaciously from the star-bespangled sky, while her light irrigated the smooth and shiny sides and wings and backs of the Blue-Bottle-Flies with a peculiar and trivial splendour, while all nature cheerfully responded to the cerulæan and conspicuous circumstances.

In many long-after years, the four little Travellers looked back to that evening as one of the happiest in all their lives, and it was already past midnight, when—the sail of the boat having been set up by the Quangle-Wangle, the Tea-kettle and Churn placed in their respective positions, and the Pussy-Cat stationed at the helm—the Children each took a last and affection-ate farewell of the Blue-Bottle-Flies, who walked down in a body to the water's edge to see the Travellers embark.

As a token of parting respect and esteem,

Violet made a curtsey quite down to the ground, and stuck one of her few remaining Parrot-tail

feathers into the back hair of the most pleasing of the Blue-Bottle-Flies, while Slingsby, Guy, and Lionel offered them three small boxes, containing respectively Black Pins, Dried Figs, and Epsom Salts ; and thus they left that happy shore for ever.

Overcome by their feelings, the four little Travellers instantly jumped into the Tea-kettle, and fell fast asleep. But all along the shore for many hours there was distinctly heard a sound of severely suppressed sobs, and a vague multitude of living creatures using their pocket-handker-chiefs in a subdued simultaneous snuffle—

lingering sadly along the wallopping waves, as
the boat sailed farther and farther away from the
Land of the Happy Blue-Bottle-Flies.

Nothing particular occurred for some days
after these events, except that as the Travellers
were passing a low tract of sand, they perceived
an unusual and gratifying spectacle, namely, a
large number of Crabs and Crawfish—perhaps
six or seven hundred—sitting by the waterside,
and endeavouring to disentangle a vast heap of
pale pink worsted, which they moistened at
intervals with a fluid composed of Lavender-
water and White-wine Negus.

" Can we be of any service to you, O crusty
Crabbies ? " said the Four Children.

" Thank you kindly," said the Crabs, con-
secutively.   " We are trying to make some
worsted Mittens, but do not know how."

On which Violet, who was perfectly acquainted
with the art of mitten-making, said to the Crabs,
" Do your claws unscrew, or are they fixtures ? "

" They are all made to unscrew," said the

Crabs, and forthwith they deposited a great pile of claws close to the boat, with which Violet uncombed all the pale pink worsted, and then made the loveliest Mittens with it you can imagine. These the Crabs, having resumed and screwed on their claws, placed cheerfully upon their wrists, and walked away rapidly, on their hind legs, warbling songs with a silvery voice and in a minor key.

After this the four little people sailed on again till they came to a vast and wide plain of astonishing dimensions, on which nothing whatever could be discovered at first; but as the Travellers walked onward, there appeared in the extreme and dim distance a single object, which on a nearer approach, and on an accurately cutaneous inspection, seemed to be somebody in a large white wig sitting on an arm-chair made of Sponge Cakes and Oyster-shells. "It does not quite look like a human being," said Violet doubtfully; nor could they make out what it really was, till the Quangle-Wangle (who had previously been round the world) exclaimed softly in a loud voice, "It is the Co-operative Cauliflower!"

And so in truth it was, and they soon found that what they had taken for an immense wig was in reality the top of the cauliflower, and that he had no feet at all, being able to walk tolerably well with a fluctuating and graceful movement on a single cabbage stalk, an accomplishment which naturally saved him the expense of stockings and shoes.

Presently, while the whole party from the boat was gazing at him with mingled affection and disgust, he suddenly arose, and in a somewhat plumdomphious manner hurried off towards the setting sun,—his steps supported by two super-incumbent confidential cucumbers, and a large number of Waterwagtails proceeding in advance of him by three-and-three in a row,—till he

finally disappeared on the brink of the western sky in a crystal cloud of sudorific sand.

So remarkable a sight of course impressed the Four Children very deeply; and they returned immediately to their boat with a strong sense of undeveloped asthma and a great appetite.

Shortly after this the Travellers were obliged to sail directly below some high overhanging rocks, from the top of one of which a particularly odious little boy, dressed in rose-coloured knickerbockers, and with a pewter plate upon his head, threw an enormous Pumpkin at the boat, by which it was instantly upset.

But this upsetting was of no consequence, because all the party knew how to swim very

well, and in fact they preferred swimming about
till after the moon rose, when, the water growing
chilly, they sponge-taneously entered the boat.
Meanwhile the Quangle-Wangle threw back the
Pumpkin with immense force, so that it hit the

rocks where the malicious little boy in rose-
coloured knickerbockers was sitting, when, being
quite full of Lucifer-matches, the Pumpkin
exploded surreptitiously into a thousand bits,
whereon the rocks instantly took fire, and the
odious little boy became unpleasantly hotter and

hotter and hotter, till his knickerbockers were turned quite green, and his nose was burned off.

Two or three days after this had happened they came to another place, where they found nothing at all except some wide and deep pits full of Mulberry Jam. This is the property of the tiny Yellow-nosed Apes who abound in these districts, and who store up the Mulberry Jam for their food in winter, when they mix it with pellucid pale periwinkle soup, and serve it out in Wedgwood China bowls, which grow freely all over that part of the country. Only one of the Yellow-nosed Apes was on the spot, and he was fast asleep; yet the Four Travellers and the Quangle-Wangle and Pussy were so terrified by the violence and sanguinary sound of his snoring, that they merely took a small cupful of the Jam, and returned to re-embark in their boat without delay.

What was their horror on seeing the boat (including the Churn and the Tea-kettle) in the mouth of an enormous Seeze Pyder, an aquatic and ferocious creature truly dreadful to behold, and happily only met with in those excessive longitudes. In a moment the beautiful boat was bitten into fifty-five-thousand-million-hundred-

billion bits ; and it instantly became quite clear that Violet, Slingsby, Guy, and Lionel could no longer preliminate their voyage by sea.

The Four Travellers were therefore obliged to resolve on pursuing their wanderings by land, and very fortunately there happened to pass by at that moment an elderly Rhinoceros, on which they seized ; and all four mounting on his back, the Quangle-Wangle sitting on his horn and holding on by his ears, and the Pussy-Cat swinging at the end of his tail, they set off, having only four small beans and three pounds

of mashed potatoes to last through their whole journey.

They were, however, able to catch numbers of the chickens and turkeys and other birds who incessantly alighted on the head of the Rhinoceros for the purpose of gathering the seeds of the rhododendron plants which grew there, and these creatures they cooked in the most translucent and satisfactory manner, by means of a fire lighted on the end of the Rhinoceros's back. A crowd of Kangaroos and Gigantic Cranes accompanied them, from feelings of curiosity and complacency, so that they were never at a loss for company, and went onward as it were in a sort of profuse and triumphant procession.

Thus, in less than eighteen weeks, they all arrived safely at home, where they were received by their admiring relatives with joy tempered with contempt; and where they finally resolved to carry out the rest of their travelling plans at some more favourable opportunity.

As for the Rhinoceros, in token of their grateful adherence, they had him killed and stuffed directly, and then set him up outside the door of their father's house as a Diaphanous Doorscraper.

THE HISTORY OF THE SEVEN FAMILIES OF THE LAKE PIPPLE-POPPLE

CHAPTER I

INTRODUCTORY

IN former days—that is to say, once upon a time, there lived in the Land of Gramblamble, Seven Families. They lived by the side of the great Lake Pipple-Popple (one of the Seven Families, indeed, lived *in* the Lake), and on the outskirts of the City of Tosh, which, excepting when it was quite dark, they could see plainly. The names of all these places you have probably heard of, and you have only not to look in your Geography books to find out all about them.

Now the Seven Families who lived on the borders of the great Lake Pipple-Popple, were as follows in the next Chapter.

CHAPTER II
THE SEVEN FAMILIES

THERE was a family of Two old Parrots and
Seven young Parrots.

There was a family of Two old Storks and
Seven young Storks.

N

There was a Family of Two old Geese and
Seven young Geese.

There was a Family of Two old Owls and
Seven young Owls.

There was a Family of Two old Guinea Pigs
and Seven young Guinea Pigs.

There was a Family of Two old Cats and Seven young Cats.

And there was a Family of Two old Fishes and Seven young Fishes.

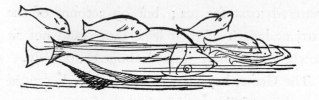

CHAPTER III

THE HABITS OF THE SEVEN FAMILIES

THE Parrots lived upon the Soffsky-Poffsky trees,—which were beautiful to behold, and covered with blue leaves,—and they fed upon fruit, artichokes, and striped beetles.

The Storks walked in and out of the Lake Pipple-Popple and ate frogs for breakfast and buttered toast for tea; but on account of the extreme length of their legs, they could not sit down, and so they walked about continually.

The Geese, having webs to their feet, caught quantities of flies, which they ate for dinner.

The Owls anxiously looked after mice, which they caught and made into sago puddings.

The Guinea Pigs toddled about the gardens, and ate lettuces and Cheshire cheese.

The Cats sate still in the sunshine, and fed upon sponge biscuits.

The Fishes lived in the Lake, and fed chiefly on boiled periwinkles.

And all these Seven Families lived together in the utmost fun and felicity.

CHAPTER IV

THE CHILDREN OF THE SEVEN FAMILIES ARE
SENT AWAY

ONE day all the Seven Fathers and the Seven Mothers of the Seven Families agreed that they would send their children out to see the world.

So they called them all together, and gave them each eight shillings and some good advice, some chocolate drops, and a small green morocco pocket-book to set down their expenses in.

They then particularly entreated them not to quarrel, and all the parents sent off their children with a parting injunction.

" If," said the old Parrots, " you find a Cherry, do not fight about who shall have it."

" And," said the old Storks, " if you find a Frog, divide it carefully into seven bits, and on no account quarrel about it."

And the old Geese said to the Seven young

Geese, " Whatever you do, be sure you do not touch a Plum-pudding Flea."

And the old Owls said, " If you find a Mouse, tear him up into seven slices, and eat him cheerfully, but without quarrelling."

And the old Guinea Pigs said, " Have a care that you eat your Lettuces, should you find any, not greedily but calmly."

And the old Cats said, " Be particularly careful not to meddle with a Clangle-Wangle, if you should see one."

And the old Fishes said, " Above all things avoid eating a blue Boss-Woss, for they do not agree with Fishes, and give them a pain in their toes."

So all the Children of each Family thanked their parents, and making in all forty-nine polite bows, they went into the wide world.

CHAPTER V

THE HISTORY OF THE SEVEN YOUNG PARROTS

THE Seven young Parrots had not gone far, when they saw a tree with a single Cherry on it, which the oldest Parrot picked instantly, but the other six being extremely hungry, tried to get it also. On which all the Seven began to fight, and they scuffled,

and huffled,

and ruffled,

and shuffled,

and puffled,

and muffled,

and buffled,

and duffled,

and fluffled,

and guffled,

and bruffled, and screamed, and shrieked, and squealed, and squeaked, and clawed, and snapped, and bit, and bumped, and thumped, and dumped, and flumped each other, till they were all torn into little bits, and at last there was nothing left to record this painful incident, except the Cherry and seven small green feathers.

And that was the vicious and voluble end of the Seven young Parrots.

CHAPTER VI

THE HISTORY OF THE SEVEN YOUNG STORKS

WHEN the Seven young Storks set out, they walked or flew for fourteen weeks in a straight line, and for six weeks more in a crooked one; and after that they ran as hard as they could for one hundred and eight miles; and after that they stood still and made a himmeltanious chatter-clatter-blattery noise with their bills.

About the same time they perceived a large Frog, spotted with green, and with a sky-blue stripe under each ear.

So being hungry, they immediately flew at him and were going to divide him into seven pieces, when they began to quarrel as to which of his legs should be taken off first. One said this, and another said that, and while they were all quarrelling the Frog hopped away. And when they saw that he was gone, they began to chatter-clatter,

   blatter-platter,

     patter-blatter,

       matter-clatter,

         flatter-quatter, more violently than ever. And after they had fought for a week they pecked each other to little pieces, so that at last nothing was left of any of them except their bills.

And that was the end of the Seven young Storks.

CHAPTER VII

THE HISTORY OF THE SEVEN YOUNG GEESE

WHEN the Seven young Geese began to travel, they went over a large plain, on which there was but one tree, and that was a very bad one.

So four of them went up to the top of it, and looked about them, while the other three waddled up and down, and repeated poetry, and their last six lessons in Arithmetic, Geography, and Cookery.

Presently they perceived, a long way off, an object of the most interesting and obese appearance, having a perfectly round body, exactly resembling a boiled plum-pudding, with two little wings, and a beak, and three feathers growing out of his head, and only one leg.

So after a time all the Seven young Geese said to each other, " Beyond all doubt this beast must be a Plum-pudding Flea ! "

On which they incautiously began to sing aloud,

"Plum-pudding Flea,

"Plum-pudding Flea,

"Wherever you be,

"O come to our tree,

"And listen, O listen, O listen to me!"

And no sooner had they sung this verse than the Plum-pudding Flea began to hop and skip on his one leg with the most dreadful velocity, and came straight to the tree, where he stopped and looked about him in a vacant and voluminous manner.

On which the Seven young Geese were greatly alarmed, and all of a tremble-bemble : so one of them put out his long neck and just touched him with the tip of his bill,—but no sooner had he done this than the Plum-pudding Flea skipped and hopped about more and more and higher and higher, after which he opened his mouth, and to the great surprise and indignation of the Seven Geese, began to bark so loudly and

furiously and terribly that they were totally
unable to bear the noise, and by degrees every
one of them suddenly tumbled down quite dead.

So that was the end of the Seven young Geese.

CHAPTER VIII

The History of the Seven Young Owls

WHEN the Seven young Owls set out, they sat every now and then on the branches of old trees, and never went far at one time.

And one night when it was quite dark, they thought they heard a mouse, but as the gas lamps were not lighted, they could not see him.

So they called out, " Is that a mouse ? "

On which a Mouse answered, " Squeaky-peeky-weeky, yes it is."

And immediately all the young Owls threw themselves off the tree, meaning to alight on the ground ; but they did not perceive that there was a large well below them, into which they all fell superficially, and were every one of them drowned in less than half a minute.

So that was the end of the Seven young Owls.

CHAPTER IX

The History of the Seven Young Guinea Pigs

THE Seven young Guinea Pigs went into a garden full of Gooseberry-bushes and Tiggory-trees, under one of which they fell asleep. When they awoke they saw a large Lettuce which had grown out of the ground while they had been sleeping, and which had an immense number of green leaves. At which they all exclaimed,

"Lettuce! O Lettuce!

"Let us, O let us,

"O Lettuce leaves,

"O let us leave this tree and eat

"Lettuce, O let us, Lettuce leaves!"

And instantly the Seven young Guinea Pigs rushed with such extreme force against the Lettuce-plant, and hit their heads so vividly against its stalk, that the concussion brought on directly an incipient transitional inflammation of their noses, which grew worse and worse and worse and worse till it incidentally killed them all Seven.

And that was the end of the Seven young Guinea Pigs.

CHAPTER X

THE HISTORY OF THE SEVEN YOUNG CATS

THE Seven young Cats set off on their travels with great delight and rapacity. But, on coming to the top of a high hill, they perceived at a long distance off a Clangle-Wangle (or, as it is more properly written, Clangel-Wangel), and in spite of the warning they had had, they ran straight up to it.

(Now the Clangle-Wangle is a most dangerous and delusive beast, and by no means commonly to be met with. They live in the water as well as on land, using their long tail as a sail when in the former element. Their speed is extreme, but their habits of life are domestic and superfluous, and their general demeanour pensive and pellucid. On summer evenings they may sometimes be observed near the Lake Pipple-Popple, standing on their heads and humming their national melodies : they subsist entirely on vegetables, excepting when they eat veal, or mutton, or pork, or beef, or fish, or saltpetre.)

The moment the Clangle-Wangle saw the Seven young Cats approach, he ran away; and as he ran straight on for four months, and the Cats, though they continued to run, could never overtake him,—they all gradually *died* of fatigue and exhaustion, and never afterwards recovered.

And this was the end of the Seven young Cats.

CHAPTER XI

THE HISTORY OF THE SEVEN YOUNG FISHES

THE Seven young Fishes swam across the Lake Pipple-Popple, and into the river, and into the ocean, where most unhappily for them they saw, on the fifteenth day of their travels, a bright-blue Boss-Woss, and instantly swam after him. But the Blue Boss-Woss plunged into a perpendicular,

spicular,

orbicular,

quadrangular,

circular depth of soft mud,

where in fact his house was.

And the Seven young Fishes, swimming with great and uncomfortable velocity, plunged also into the mud, quite against their will, and not being accustomed to it, were all suffocated in a very short period.

And that was the end of the Seven young Fishes.

CHAPTER XII

OF WHAT OCCURRED SUBSEQUENTLY

AFTER it was known that the
Seven young Parrots,

and the Seven young Storks,

and the Seven young Geese,

and the Seven young Owls,

and the Seven young Guinea Pigs,

and the Seven young Cats,

and the Seven young Fishes,

were all dead, then the Frog, and the Plum-pudding Flea, and the Mouse, and the Clangel-Wangel, and the Blue Boss-Woss, all met together to rejoice over their good fortune.

And they collected the Seven Feathers of the Seven young Parrots, and the Seven Bills of the Seven young Storks, and the Lettuce, and the Cherry, and having placed the latter on the Lettuce, and the other objects in a circular arrangement at their base, they danced a hornpipe round all these memorials until they were quite tired; after which they gave a tea-party, and a garden-party, and a ball, and a concert, and then returned to their respective homes full of joy and respect, sympathy, satisfaction, and disgust.

Chapter XIII

Of what became of the Parents of the Forty-nine Children

BUT when the two old Parrots,
    and the two old Storks,
    and the two old Geese,
    and the two old Owls,
    and the two old Guinea Pigs,
    and the two old Cats,
    and the two old Fishes,

became aware, by reading in the newspapers, of the calamitous extinction of the whole of their families, they refused all further sustenance; and sending out to various shops, they purchased great quantities of Cayenne Pepper, and Brandy, and Vinegar, and blue Sealing-wax, besides Seven immense glass Bottles with air-tight stoppers. And having done this, they ate a light supper of brown bread and Jerusalem Artichokes, and took an affecting and formal leave of the whole of their acquaintance, which was very numerous and distinguished, and select, and responsible, and ridiculous.

CHAPTER XIV

CONCLUSION

AND after this, they filled the bottles with
the ingredients for pickling, and each
couple jumped into a separate bottle, by which
effort of course they all died immediately, and
became thoroughly pickled in a few minutes;
having previously made their wills (by the
assistance of the most eminent Lawyers of the
District), in which they left strict orders that the
Stoppers of the Seven Bottles should be carefully
sealed up with the blue Sealing-wax they had
purchased; and that they themselves in the
Bottles should be presented to the principal
museum of the city of Tosh, to be labelled with
Parchment or any other anti-congenial succe-
daneum, and to be placed on a marble table with
silver-gilt legs, for the daily inspection and
contemplation, and for the perpetual benefit of
the pusillanimous public.

And if ever you happen to go to Gramble-Blamble, and visit that museum in the city of Tosh, look for them on the Ninety-eighth table in the Four hundred and twenty-seventh room of the right-hand corridor of the left wing of the Central Quadrangle of that magnificent building ; for if you do not, you certainly will not see them.

NONSENSE ALPHABETS

A

a

A was once an Apple-pie,

> Pidy
>
> Widy
>
> Tidy
>
> Pidy
>
> Nice insidy
>
> Apple-pie.

B

b

B was once a little Bear,

Beary!

Wary!

Hairy!

Beary!

Taky cary!

Little Bear!

C

c

C was once a little Cake,

> Caky,
> Baky
> Maky
> Caky,
> Taky Caky,
> Little Cake.

o

D

d

D was once a little Doll,

Dolly,

Molly,

Polly,

Nolly,

Nursy Dolly

Little Doll!

E

e

E was once a little Eel,

> Eely
> Weely
> Peely
> Eely
> Twirly, Tweely,
> Little Eel.

F

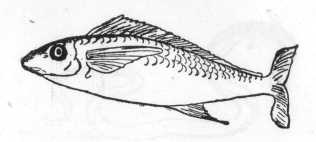

f

F was once a little Fish,

Fishy

Wishy

Squishy

Fishy

In a Dishy

Little Fish !

G

g

G was once a little Goose,

    Goosy

    Moosy

    Boosey

    Goosey

    Waddly woosy

    Little Goose !

H

h

H was once a little Hen,

> Henny
> Chenny
> Tenny
> Henny
> Eggsy-any
> Little Hen?

I

i

I was once a Bottle of Ink,

> Inky
> Dinky
> Thinky
> Inky,
> Blacky Minky
> Bottle of Ink!

J

j

J was once a Jar of Jam,

Jammy
Mammy
Clammy
Jammy
Sweety—Swammy
Jar of Jam!

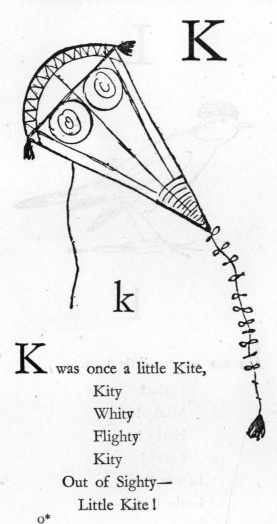

K

k

K was once a little Kite,
  Kity
  Whity
  Flighty
  Kity
 Out of Sighty—
  Little Kite !

o*

L

l

L was once a little Lark,

> Larky!
> Marky!
> Harky!
> Larky!
> In the Parky,
> Little Lark!

M

m

M was once a little Mouse,

> Mousey
> Bousey
> Sousy
> Mousy
> In the Housy
> Little Mouse !

N

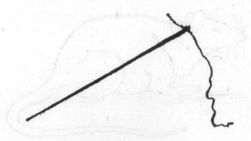

n

N was once a little Needle,

> Needly
> Tweedly
> Threedly
> Needly
> Wisky—wheedly
> Little Needle !

O was once a little Owl,

    Owly
    Prowly
    Howly
    Owly
    Browny Fowly
    Little Owl !

P

P was once a little Pump,

> Pumpy
> Slumpy
> Flumpy
> Pumpy
> Dumpy, Thumpy
> Little Pump!

Q

q

Q was once a little Quail,

> Quaily
> Faily
> Daily
> Quaily
> Stumpy-taily
> Little Quail !

R

r

R was once a little Rose,

Rosy
Posy
Nosy
Rosy
Blows-y—grows-y
Little Rose!

S

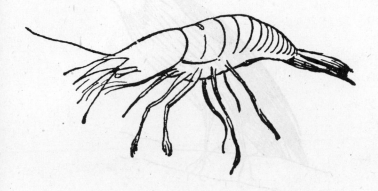

s

S was once a little Shrimp,

> Shrimpy
> Nimpy
> Flimpy
> Shrimpy
> Jumpy—jimpy
> Little Shrimp!

T

t

T was once a little Thrush,

Thrushy
Hushy
Bushy
Thrushy
Flitty—Flushy
Little Thrush !

U

u

U was once a little Urn,

> Urny
>
> Burny
>
> Turny
>
> Urny
>
> Bubbly—burny
>
> Little Urn.

V

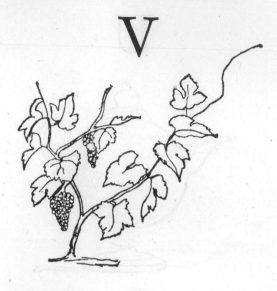

V

V was once a little Vine.

> Viny
> Winy
> Twiny
> Viny
> Twisty-twiny
> Little Vine!

W

W

W was once a Whale,
> Whaly
> Scaly
> Shaly
> Whaly
> Tumbly-taily
> Mighty Whale!

X

X

X was once a great King Xerxes,

Xerxy
Perxy
Turxy
Xerxy
Linxy I urxy
Great King Xerxes!

Y

y

Y was once a little Yew,
Yewdy
Fewdy
Crudy
Yewdy
Growdy, grewdy,
Little Yew!

Z

z

Z was once a piece of Zinc,

  Tinky
  Winky
  Blinky
  Tinky
  Tinkly Minky
  Piece of Zinc!

A

A was an Ape,
Who stole some white Tape,
And tied up his Toes
In four beautiful Bows.

a

Funny old Ape!

B

B was a Bat,
Who slept all the Day,
And fluttered about,
When the Sun went away.

b

Brown little Bat!

C

C was a Camel,
You rode on his Hump,
And if you fell off,
You came down such a Bump!

C

What a high Camel!

D

D was a Dove
Who lived in a Wood,
With such pretty soft Wings,
And so gentle and good.

d

Dear little Dove!

E

E was an Eagle
Who sate on the Rocks,
And looked down on the Fields
And the far-away Flocks.

e

Beautiful Eagle !

F

F was a Fan
Made of beautiful Stuff,
And when it was used
It went—Puffy-puff-puff!

f

Nice little Fan.

G

G was a Gooseberry,
Perfectly Red ;
To be made into jam
And eaten with Bread.

g

Gooseberry Red !

H was a Heron,
Who stood in a Stream,
The length of his Neck
And his Legs was extreme!

h

Long-legged Heron!

I

I was an Inkstand
Which stood on a Table
With a nice Pen to write with,
When we are able!

i

Neat little Inkstand!

P

J

J was a Jug,
So pretty and white,
With fresh Water in it
At morning and night.

j

Nice little Jug!

K

K was a Kingfisher,
Quickly he flew,
So bright and so pretty
Green, Purple, and Blue.

k

Kingfisher, Blue!

L

L was a Lily
So white and so sweet,
To see it and smell it
Was quite a nice treat!

1

Beautiful Lily!

M

M was a Man
Who walked round and round
And he wore a long Coat
That came down to the Ground.

m

Funny old Man!

N

N was a Nut
So smooth and so brown,
And when it was ripe
It fell tumble-dum-down.

n

Nice little Nut !

O

O was an Oyster
Who lived in his Shell,
If you let him alone
He felt perfectly well.

O

Open-mouth'd Oyster !

P

P was a Polly,
All red, blue, and green,
The most beautiful Polly
That ever was seen.

P

Poor little Polly!

Q

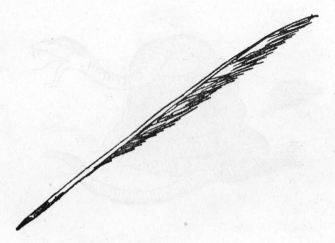

Q was a Quill
Made into a Pen,
But I do not know where
And I cannot say when.

q

Nice little Quill!

P*

R

R was a Rattlesnake
Rolled up so tight,
Those who saw him ran quickly
For fear he should bite.

r

Rattlesnake bite!

S

S was a Screw
To screw down a box,
And then it was fastened
Without any locks.

S

Valuable Screw!

T

T was a Thimble
Of silver so bright,
When placed on the finger
It fitted so tight!

t

Nice little Thimble!

U

U was an Upper-coat
Woolly and warm,
To wear over all
In the snow or the storm.

u

What a nice Upper-coat!

V

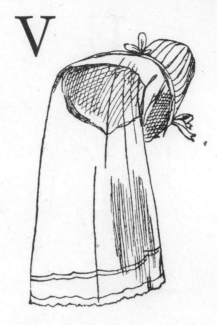

V was a Veil

With a border upon it,
And a riband to tie it
All round a pink bonnet.

V

Pretty green Veil!

W

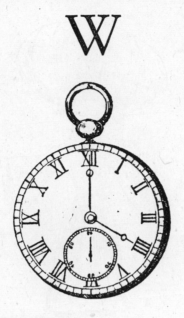

W was a Watch,
Where in letters of gold
The hour of the day
You might always behold.

W

Beautiful Watch!

X

X was King Xerxes,
Who wore on his head
A mighty large Turban,
Green, yellow, and red.

X

Look at King Xerxes!

Y

Y was a Yak
From the land of Thibet,
Except his white Tail
He was all black as jet.

y

Look at the Yak!

Z

Z was a Zebra
All striped white and black,
And if he were tame
You might ride on his back.

Z

Pretty striped Zebra!

ALPHABET

—

A tumbled down, and hurt his Arm, against a bit of wood.

B said, "My Boy, O! do not cry; it cannot do you good!"

C said, "A Cup of Coffee hot can't do you any harm."

D said, "A Doctor should be fetched, and he would cure the arm."

E said, "An Egg beat up with milk would quickly make him well."

F said, "A Fish, if broiled, might cure, if only by the smell."

G said, " Green Gooseberry fool, the best of cures I hold."

H said, " His Hat should be kept on, to keep him from the cold."

I said, " Some Ice upon his head will make him better soon."

J said, " Some Jam, if spread on bread, or given in a spoon ! "

K said, " A Kangaroo is here,—this picture let him see."

L said, " A Lamp pray keep alight, to make some barley tea."

M said, " A Mulberry or two might give him satisfaction."

N said, " Some Nuts, if rolled about, might be a slight attraction."

O said, " An Owl might make him laugh, if only it would wink."

P said, " Some Poetry might be read aloud, to make him think."

Q said, " A Quince I recommend,—a Quince, or else a Quail."

R said, " Some Rats might make him move, if fastened by their tail."

S said, " A Song should now be sung, in hopes to make him laugh ! "

T said, " A Turnip might avail, if sliced or cut in half ! "

U said, " An Urn, with water hot, place underneath his chin ! "

V said, " I'll stand upon a chair, and play a Violin ! "

W said, "Some Whisky-Whizzgigs fetch,
some marbles and a ball!"

X said, "Some double XX ale would be the
best of all!"

Y said, "Some Yeast mixed up with salt
would make a perfect plaster!"

Z said, "Here is a box of Zinc! Get in, my
little master!
"We'll shut you up! We'll nail you down!
We will, my little master!
"We think we've all heard quite enough
of this your sad disaster!"

NONSENSE COOKERY

THREE RECEIPTS FOR DOMESTIC COOKERY

To Make an Amblongus Pie

TAKE 4 pounds (say 4½ pounds) of fresh Amblongusses, and put them in a small pipkin.

Cover them with water and boil them for 8 hours incessantly, after which add 2 pints of new milk, and proceed to boil for 4 hours more.

When you have ascertained that the Amblongusses are quite soft, take them out and place them in a wide pan, taking care to shake them well previously.

Grate some nutmeg over the surface, and cover them carefully with powdered gingerbread, curry-powder, and a sufficient quantity of cayenne pepper.

Remove the pan into the next room, and place it on the floor. Bring it back again, and let it simmer for three-quarters of an hour. Shake the pan violently till all the Amblongusses have become of a pale purple colour.

Then, having prepared the paste, insert the whole carefully, adding at the same time a small pigeon, 2 slices of beef, 4 cauliflowers, and any number of oysters.

Watch patiently till the crust begins to rise, and add a pinch of salt from time to time.

Serve up in a clean dish, and throw the whole out of the window as fast as possible.

To Make Crumbobblious Cutlets

PROCURE some strips of beef, and having cut them into the smallest possible slices, proceed to cut them still smaller, eight or perhaps nine times.

When the whole is thus minced, brush it up hastily with a new clothes-brush, and stir round rapidly and capriciously with a salt-spoon or a soup-ladle.

Place the whole in a saucepan, and remove it to a sunny place,—say the roof of the house if free from sparrows or other birds,—and leave it there for about a week.

At the end of that time add a little lavender, some oil of almonds, and a few herring-bones; and then cover the whole with 4 gallons of clarified crumbobblious sauce, when it will be ready for use.

Cut it into the shape of ordinary cutlets, and serve up in a clean tablecloth or dinner-napkin.

To Make Gosky Patties

TAKE a Pig, three or four years of age, and tie him by the off hind leg to a post. Place 5 pounds of currants, 3 of sugar, 2 pecks of peas, 18 roast chestnuts, a candle, and 6 bushels of turnips, within his reach; if he eats these, constantly provide him with more.

Then procure some cream, some slices of Cheshire cheese, four quires of foolscap paper, and a packet of black pins. Work the whole into a paste, and spread it out to dry on a sheet of clean brown waterproof linen.

When the paste is perfectly dry, but not before, proceed to beat the Pig violently, with the handle of a large broom. If he squeals, beat him again.

Visit the paste and beat the Pig alternately for some days, and ascertain if at the end of that period the whole is about to turn into Gosky Patties.

If it does not then, it never will; and in that case the Pig may be let loose, and the whole process may be considered as finished.

THE HERALDIC BLAZON OF
FOSS THE CAT

Foſs Couchant

Foſs, a untin.

Fos
rampant

Fos dansant

Shape Shifter
Transform Your Life in 1 Day

Geoff Thompson

£7.99 P/b

ISBN: 1-84024-444-5

ISBN 13: 978-1-84024-444-1

What if you could become anything you wanted? What if there was a method of practice that allowed ordinary men and women to transform themselves into beings of extraordinary talent?

It is a commonly held belief that the leading lights of society are gifted from birth or just plain lucky, but Geoff Thompson believes that anyone with average ability and a strong desire can succeed in any chosen field. The ex-bouncer and factory floor sweeper, now a martial arts expert, screenwriter, Bafta-award winning film-maker and author of 30 books, knows this better than most. In *Shape Shifter*, the first self-help guide of its kind, you will learn:

- That shape shifting is our birthright as a creative species

- How to practise the art of personal transformation, step by step

- That with the right strategy and approach, success is always a choice

www.summersdale.com

www.geoffthompson.com

Foss, regardant

Foss Pprpr.

LIST OF LEAR'S WORKS

The following is a list of Edward Lear's principal works. Much of his early work in animal drawing was done as illustration for other authors.

"Illustrations of the Family of the Psittacidæ," 1832.

"Tortoises, Terrapins, and Turtles," by J. E. Gray, drawn from life by Sowerby and Lear.

"Views in Rome and its Environs," 1841.

"Gleanings from the Menagerie at Knowsley Hall," 1846.

"Illustrated Excursions in Italy," 1846.

"Book of Nonsense," 1846.

"Journal of a Landscape Painter in Greece and Albania," 1851.

"Journal of a Landscape Painter in Southern Albania," 1852.

"Book of Nonsense and More Nonsense," 1862.

"Views in the Seven Ionian Isles," 1863.

"Journal of a Landscape Painter in Corsica," 1870.

"Nonsense Songs and Stories," 1871.

"More Nonsense Songs, Pictures, etc.," 1872.

"Laughable Lyrics," 1877.

"Nonsense Alphabets."

"Nonsense Botany," 1888.

".Tennyson's Poems, illustrated by Lear," 1889.

"Facsimile of a Nonsense Alphabet," done in 1849, but published for the first time in a limited edition, 1926.

Printed for the Publishers by Butler & Tanner Ltd., Frome and London
745.1047